LEADERSHIP ALCHEMY

ESSENTIAL TRUTHS FOR DRIVING TRANSFORMATIONAL CHANGE

MICHAEL CORVINI, MD, MBA

ISBN: 979-8-89079-478-9 (hardcover)
ISBN: 979-8-89079-479-6 (paperback)
ISBN: 979-8-89079-480-2 (ebook)

TABLE OF CONTENTS

PART ONE:
DISCOVERING ALLEGORICAL WISDOM

PART TWO:
EXPLORING THE ESSENTIAL
LEADERSHIP TRUTHS

INTRODUCTION

This is my first book. I chose to independently publish it because most publishers would have advised against beginning it this way. And they probably would have objected to making the following question the premise of the Introduction. But I've found that leadership could use a bit more humility and lightheartedness. So here we go:

What do ski lifts have in common with bar stools and confessionals?

The superficial answer is that they're all places to sit. The deeper answer is that they all have the ability to evoke truth. Of the three, ski lifts may be the least recognized for this quality, but they are undeniably effective.

I'd like to believe this is due to a combination of transcendental factors: the clarifying mountain air, the disarming beauty of nature, and the symbolism of rising to greater heights. Yet the reason is likely simpler. They offer a short ride with someone you will never see again. Why not tell them the unvarnished truth?

I've ridden countless ski lifts and heard all kinds of things along the way—most mundane, but some quite profound. On one remarkable ride in Telluride, Colorado, I was told an essential truth about leadership.

NURSE BONNIE

Telluride is rarely crowded, especially at ski lift number nine. So it's not unusual to share the four-passenger chair with only one other rider. On this occasion, my companion was a nurse named Bonnie. She was wearing an audaciously cheerful outfit, but her facial expression said the opposite. Curious about the contrast, I asked how her day was going. Her bitterness was unmistakable as she declared that "every day on the slopes—and not at work—is a good day." Naturally, that caused me to ask what she did for work. She told me she was a nurse and hated it. When I asked why, she shared that throughout her 30-year career she had found that "too many hospitals did a bad job." She had an extensive list of what constituted "bad" and conveyed it with sulfuric vitriol.

While I didn't share her cynicism, I was genuinely interested in her perspective. I asked if any of the hospitals had done an outstanding job. She softened and admitted that several had. When I asked what they had in common, her response was immediate—they had "good leadership." As we neared the top, I posed one final question. What made the leadership "good?" Her answer: "Beyond all the practical bullsh*t of running a hospital, good leadership always comes down to two simple things." She quickly disclosed them before we skied off.

In naming those "two simple things," Bonnie had revealed a profound and essential truth about leadership.

ON THE HISTORY OF LEADERSHIP BOOKS

The earliest systematic treatise on leadership in Western culture is generally considered to be the *Cyropaedia*, written by the Greek soldier and historian Xenophon around 370 BCE.[1,2] It's a comprehensive exposition of Cyrus the Great and uses his example as a template for effective leadership. Xenophon covers the themes of self-mastery, moral character, humility, discipline, and sound decision-making. He emphasizes leading by example, motivating and influencing followers, and grounding authority in voluntary obedience. He also addresses cultural awareness, adaptability, structure, strategy, accountability, succession planning, justice, and service. Like I said—it was comprehensive.[1,2,3,4,5]

In the roughly 2,400 years that have followed, the study of leadership has spanned the sectors of philosophy, psychology, business, politics, the military, and countless other disciplines. Each has added perspective and nuance, shaping how we think about leadership today.

Yet when the central tenets of the *Cyropaedia* are compared to those of contemporary leadership, the differences are surprisingly small—centered primarily on checks and balances, follower empowerment, psychological safety, and emotional intelligence.[1,6,7] Considering that most of these concepts didn't emerge until the mid-1990s, it's noteworthy that it took more than two millennia for something "new" to come along. And in the three decades since these concepts appeared, at least another 60,000 books on leadership have been published in the United States alone, with the pace of publication continuing to increase.

WHY THIS BOOK?

At this point, you might be asking if the world really needs another book on leadership. What could possibly be "new" about this one? The answer is that nothing will be new. In fact, this book is grounded in the belief that the greatest leadership mysteries are not novel—they are enduring. The value of this work, then, will not be found in any shiny new theories. Instead, it will reside in the fact that the highest truths, both in life and leadership, are so simple that they are often overlooked, misunderstood, or obscured by unnecessary complexity.

When I describe these truths as "simple," I don't mean to suggest they are unrefined or ordinary. On the contrary, I mean nothing short of sublime and transcendent. Such rarefied simplicity can be exceedingly difficult to grasp and even harder to apply. This book is designed to meet this challenge by helping you develop a profound understanding of these truths and a practical way to apply them. So while it won't furnish you with anything "new," it will provide you with something exceptionally useful.

To accomplish this, I'll begin by telling you the allegorical story of the Master Alchemist. Hidden within it are the two essential truths that Nurse Bonnie expressed as we parted ways. The rest of the book will explore these truths in detail, incorporating stories from my own experience as well as hypothetical examples to bring the concepts to life. It will also offer concrete tactics you can use to put them into practice.

As you read, I encourage you to think critically about the material. Various sections will prompt you to relate the content to your own leadership journey, turning reflection into action. For readers less familiar with allegory as a way of learning, Part One will explain how it can reveal insights that traditional methods might otherwise miss.

As you turn the final page, it's my hope that you will ski away with greater clarity and wisdom, inspired and equipped to turn lead into gold.

PART ONE

Discovering Allegorical Wisdom

1

THE STORY OF THE MASTER ALCHEMIST

Once upon a time. . .

There was a Master Alchemist who lived in seclusion.

Through years of introspection, she claimed to have discovered the secret of transmuting base metals such as lead into precious metals such as gold.

To work this miracle, she required three essential elements.

First, she required the base metal.

Second, she required something called the Elixir of Life.

Third, she required something called the Philosopher's Stone.

Regarding the base metal. . .

She claimed that it had to have the potential to become something more.

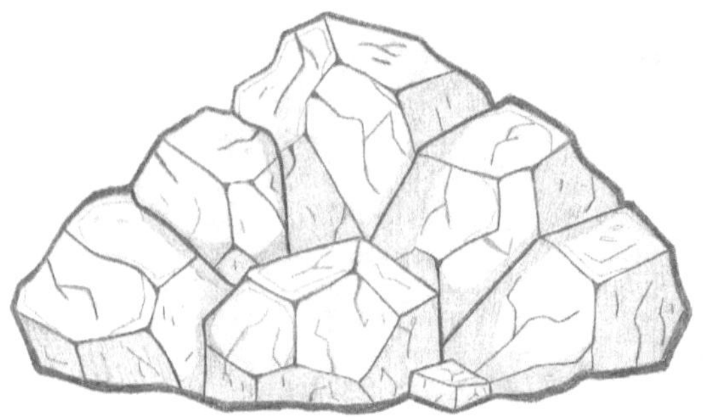

Regarding the Elixir of Life. . .

She claimed that in its pure form, it was the most powerful substance on earth.

Regarding the Philosopher's Stone. . .

She claimed that it had to be able to cause a powerful reaction.

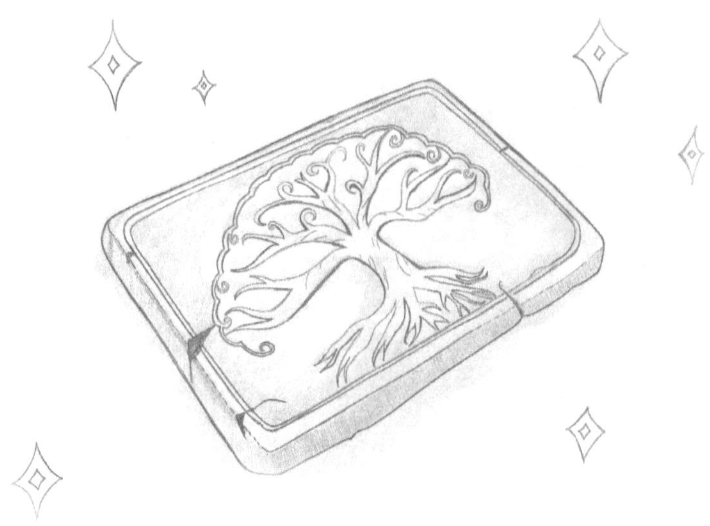

Most thought her mad, but a small number of people sought her out.

Nobody ever saw one of her trainees emerge with a horde of gold.

But none of them seemed disappointed.

In fact, they seemed quite delighted.

2
ALLEGORICAL ANALYSIS (BY THE READER)

Allegory is a form of expression that uses fictional symbolism to convey abstract ideas. It can be employed through narrative storytelling, poetry, visual art, and music. Allegorical stories typically use extended metaphor and systematic correspondence to map specific elements of the literal narrative to deeper conceptual meaning. While some make a clear and obvious connection between the literal and the figurative, others remain intentionally open-ended, leaving interpretation to the audience. As a result, a single reader may identify many valid parallels, and different readers may draw entirely different conclusions.

The story of the Master Alchemist is not something I created. It appeared across many different cultures, including ancient Greece (connected to Aristotle, 384–322 BCE), ancient Egypt (connected to Zosimos of Panopolis, 300–330 CE), the Islamic golden age (connected to Jabir ibn Hayyan, 721–815 CE), and medieval Europe (connected to Albertus Magnus, 1200–1280 CE).[8,9] These early treatments of alchemy approached it both as a literal possibility and a symbolic one.

Modern literature has continued to explore the concept of alchemy. Some examples include Johann Wolfgang von Goethe's *Faust* (1808 and 1832), Mary Shelley's *Frankenstein* (1818), and Paulo Coelho's *The Alchemist* (1988). As these other authors did in their adaptations, I took several liberties in mine, to illustrate an abstract concept that I find compellingly relevant to leadership—and which forms the foundation of this book.

In the pages that follow, I invite you to ponder the meaning of the story of the Master Alchemist by considering each surface element of the story and reflecting on what it might represent on a deeper level. Here are some suggestions to help you get the most out of the exercise:

- Remember that there is no right answer. Use introspective freedom to identify whatever the story means to you at this time in your professional life.

- Note that your insights may change if you repeat this exercise in the future.

- If you tend to think concretely and find this exercise non-intuitive, the suggestions that follow can help you use abstract thinking to uncover meaningful insights. You can also choose to skip it if you prefer.

- Take your time. Allegorical symbols are intentionally abstract, and their hidden meanings aren't immediately obvious.

- Find a quiet space, free from physical, mental, and emotional distractions. Seeking the meaning of symbols is like peering into the waters of a lake to see something far below. The surface must be as unperturbed by the ripples of literal life as possible.

- Give yourself the imaginative license to follow your musings without criticism.

- Address each element of the story in sequence. As you consider the next, draw on your earlier reflections to build a coherent symbolic narrative.

- Write down your thoughts so you don't have to worry about remembering them. I've provided ample space on the pages to come.

- If you would rather not write, you can think through the questions instead.

- Have fun with this!

What does the base metal represent?

____

15

____

What does the Elixir of Life represent?

What does the Philosopher's Stone represent?

What does the gold represent?

____

____

What does the Master Alchemist represent?

19

I hope you found that insightful. Before you continue reading, take some time to contemplate your responses. Specifically:

- What concepts do they illustrate?
- What insights do they provide?
- What lessons do they teach?
- If you were to write a book about this story, what would you want it to accomplish for the reader?

When you're ready, read on!

3
ALLEGORICAL ANALYSIS (BY THE AUTHOR)

When I first heard the story of the Master Alchemist, I found it instantly captivating. Over the years, I've reflected on its relevance to my personal and professional life and found the concepts, insights, and lessons to be transformative.

I've also found it to be a powerful teaching tool. Through its use of symbolism and layered meaning, the narrative provides a platform for exploring nuanced ideas and complex lessons that might otherwise remain elusive. It also allows the concepts to emerge gradually and resonate on a deeper level. Finally, while the story is fictional—a quality that may invite initial skepticism—it is precisely this feature that frees it from the constraints of presupposition and assumed certainty, creating space for meaningful insight. Like alchemy itself, conventionally dismissed as a fool's errand, the tale is less about the literal and more about revealing essential truths through metaphor, providing a richer understanding of leadership and the human experience.

For those who typically prefer a more concrete approach to the study of leadership, this allegorical lens may offer a refreshing complement to traditional methods. It can also build fluency in abstract thinking, enabling you to better navigate complexity by complementing practical problem-solving with conceptual strategic insight.

The remainder of this book will present an interpretation of this timeless story that I have developed into an applied leadership model called (you guessed it) Leadership Alchemy. We'll begin the journey by returning to the allegorical analysis exercise from chapter 2. This time, I will share my responses. As you read them, please remember that there is no "right answer" and that my reflections will intentionally relate to the modern-day practice of Leadership Alchemy. Accordingly, they're likely to be different from yours.

- What does the base metal represent?

  The base metal represents people and processes, yearning to be refined and elevated.

- What does the Elixir of Life represent?

  The Elixir of Life represents what I call Transformational Care. I will have more to say about this in chapter 7. For now, this isn't casual care. It is care delivered with so much intensity that it can drive transformation.

- What does the Philosopher's Stone represent?

  The Philosopher's Stone represents what I call Transformational Challenge. There will be more to come on this in chapter 8. But this isn't ordinary challenge. It is challenge, so intensely delivered, that it can trigger transformation.

- What does the gold represent?

  The gold represents people and processes, brought to their highest potential.

- What does the Master Alchemist represent?

  The Master Alchemist represents the leader who has mastered the art of using Transformational Care and Transformational Challenge to help people and processes realize their latent potential and achieve something extraordinary. It's my aim to help *you* become this Master Alchemist.

4

THE ALCHEMICAL LEADERSHIP FORMULA

Putting it all together, the story of the Master Alchemist expresses the allegorical truth that leaders are meant to be Master Alchemists who facilitate transformational change by applying the alchemical leadership formula.

The Alchemical Leadership Formula

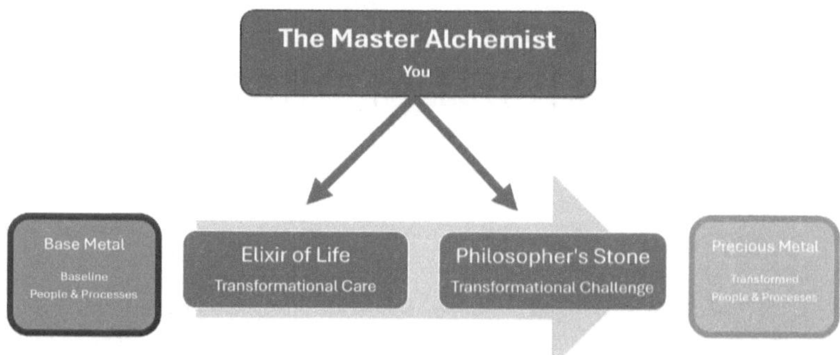

Parts Two and Three of this book will present you with a practical guide to applying this alchemical leadership formula through the contemporary practice of Leadership Alchemy. But before we "forge" ahead, it will be useful to review the history of alchemy.

5

A BRIEF HISTORY OF ALCHEMY

The earliest expositions of alchemy held that the transmutation of base metals into precious metals was theoretically possible, given the right circumstances. This notion received significant scientific skepticism in the 17th and 18th centuries with the advent of modern chemistry, giving rise to the notion of "the mad scientist."[10] The possibility of literal transmutation was definitively dismissed in the 19th century based on atomic theory.[11]

However, in the 20th century, the development of nuclear theory made the transmutation of elements theoretically possible again.[12] Eventually, particle accelerators achieved transmutation in actual practice. In the 1940s, Glenn Seaborg and colleagues used them to bombard mercury and produce gold.[13] While only a few atoms were made—and at great expense—proof of concept was established. Thereafter, several scientists used similar (exorbitantly expensive) approaches, and many precious metals were transmuted, including gold from lead.[14]

This historical reflection provides several important insights for leaders. First, our ability to accurately evaluate what's possible—and what's not—depends on our own level of understanding and development. When we make such assessments, we should remain humble about our judgments and avoid imposing our personal limitations on others. Second, what determines successful vs. unsuccessful change may be a matter of approach rather than absolute potential. In the case of alchemical transmutation, the early attempts failed because they took a chemical rather than nuclear approach. As we endeavor to lead transformative change, we must remember that taking the right approach is critical. Lastly, while we now know that it's possible to transmute base metals into precious metals, we are also aware that it comes at an absurd and impractical cost.

What, then, is the lesson of this story that has captivated people for centuries? Clearly, it isn't that we can make gold from lead. Perhaps it is that true value lies not in material possessions, but in the riches of virtue, relationship, service, and love. Perhaps it is that attempts to extract lasting worth from worldly goods will be both costly and impractical. Perhaps it is that our efforts would be better spent pursuing the transmutation of what will yield lasting treasure. And finally, perhaps once we have discovered such secrets, we should devote ourselves to helping others.

This book is based on this last supposition and is dedicated to leaders who believe it is their job to make the fictional story of the Master Alchemist a factual reality.

PART TWO
EXPLORING THE ESSENTIAL LEADERSHIP TRUTHS

6

THE MASTER ALCHEMIST: LEADING CHANGE

Once upon a time. . .

There was a Master Alchemist who lived in seclusion.

Through years of introspection, she claimed to have discovered the secret of transmuting base metals such as lead into precious metals such as gold.

Uncle Kurt

I grew up in a small town on the northeast shore of Long Island, New York. Because my family lived on several wooded acres, I was blessed with the opportunity to spend most of my free time immersed in nature. When indoors, I was usually either reading books or studying the habits of the peculiar creatures known to me as adults.

My parents had occasional dinner parties, which I found to be propitious occasions for conducting my observations. A frequent guest was my "Uncle Kurt." I put his name in quotes both because he is the subject of this story and because he earned the title through emotional rather than biological closeness.

I loved it when Uncle Kurt visited, and I imagine this was obvious from the way I would light up when he arrived and proceed to follow him around. Most people probably thought this was because he would reliably show up with a bag of jellybeans and make a big deal out of giving them to me. That didn't hurt his case. But it wasn't the jellybeans that drew me. It was something else.

Uncle Kurt genuinely cared about me. When he looked at me, his gaze was gentle yet penetrating. I could tell that he wanted to see "the me" beyond the obvious. When we spoke, he was intentional in gaining a real understanding of what I was thinking, how I was feeling, and what I was hoping for. He was curious, encouraging, and accepting, not judgmental or critical. Consequently, instead of his perspicacity making me uncomfortable, I felt respected and encouraged. Finally, he expressed genuine fondness and affection for me through his words and actions.

Uncle Kurt also challenged me. He didn't interact with me like most other adults did, watering down the exchange to be age-appropriate. He spoke in an unaffected tone, used adult vocabulary, and asked me questions about substantive topics. We then engaged in meaningful dialogue and explored my thoughts and ideas. I learned a tremendous amount from these conversations, both about life and myself. While most of the interactions were brief, they were stirring.

On one occasion, after handing me the traditional bag of jellybeans, Uncle Kurt said something like, "So, have you given thought to what you want to do when you grow up?" Now, I know this is something adults often ask children. And I understand that the question usually relates to choosing a profession. But this isn't what Uncle Kurt meant. He meant "do" in terms of how to *live life*, not "be" in terms of how to *earn a living*. Even though I was only about eight years old, I caught the distinction. I told him I wasn't sure, but I would think about it.

I left the dinner party and headed to one of my favorite places outside to contemplate the question. This happened to be a hammock strung up in a grove of maple trees. As I lay on my back, wondering what it was that I should "do" when I grew up, a gentle breeze was rustling through the trees. The leaves were that youthful, light green color of spring foliage, which seems to portray latent potential. They looked cheerful as they fluttered. I felt happy and curious, and I continued to ponder.

I would characterize all this as pleasant, but relatively ordinary. What happened next was extraordinary, and I consider it one of the greatest blessings of my life.

I was suddenly overwhelmed with a profoundly peaceful joy. Time stopped. Thought stopped. I was enraptured. I perceived this joy all around me. I felt it flowing into me and soaking me to my core. It seemed both personal and impersonal at the same time—impersonal in that I perceived that *it was as it was*, regardless of *who I was*; personal in that it seemed to be sharing itself in an affectionate way. Within this joy, I felt sublimely loved, complete, and connected to all things. I experienced an absolute sense of goodness. It was as if a veil had been lifted for me, and I was given the gift of connection with the source of this goodness. In that moment, I understood my answer to Uncle Kurt's question. What mattered in life was being connected to this goodness, learning from it, and sharing it with others.

It's hard for me to estimate how long the experience lasted, but it was probably only minutes. Once I regained my composure, I hurried inside, found my Uncle Kurt, and enthusiastically tried to explain what had happened. While I can't remember what I said, I do recall that the chatter around me stopped, and everyone listened. There were blank stares, and I felt uncomfortable. Uncle Kurt bent down, looked me in the eyes, and told me to never forget what I had just said. While his tone was light and somehow diffused the awkward silence in the room, there was gravity in what he said. I knew he understood. And he knew I understood.

For a time, I did forget what I had learned. I went on with my eight-year-old life and continued to mature. But the experience was formative. From that moment, I never believed my purpose in life was related to a specific profession: it was about striving to be a part of this grand beauty and love and offering it to others. I didn't know what to call this experience when it happened. Some might call it a religious or spiritual experience. Some, a transcendental one. Others, an epiphany. It didn't matter to me. What did matter was that it existentially changed me. I also didn't know why I had been given the blessing of the experience and still don't. But I do know that my Uncle Kurt was the catalyst. He was a Master Alchemist.

Over time, my parents lost touch with Uncle Kurt. I never got the chance to know him as an adult, to thank him for the influence he had on my life, and to find out how he became so wise. Like many of life's greatest gifts, these things will remain a mystery.

On Being a Master Alchemist

Being a Master Alchemist is dependent both on who someone is and what they do. Said another way, it requires certain personal characteristics as well as certain behaviors.

This book will focus primarily on the behaviors employed by Master Alchemists. Only chapter 9 will feature a brief exploration of their personal characteristics. This is because Leadership Alchemy is not about the Master Alchemists themselves—it's about what they do to serve others.

7

THE ELIXIR OF LIFE: DELIVERING TRANSFORMATIONAL CARE

Regarding the Elixir of Life. . .

She claimed that in its pure form, it was the most powerful substance on earth.

The Stranger

After finishing primary and high school, I attended the College of William and Mary in Williamsburg, Virginia. There, I majored in Psychology, minored in Sociology, and completed my premedical requirements. I then attended medical school at SUNY Downstate in Brooklyn, New York. I found medical school challenging in several ways.

While I had excelled in college, I was intimidated by the academic caliber of my fellow students. The sheer volume of complex material requiring both deep understanding and rote memorization was also daunting. I was afraid I would flunk out. My first battery of exams was scheduled for the end of the first semester. I prepared by waking at 5:00am on weekdays, studying until I needed to take the train to class, studying on the train, attending class, studying during lunch, studying on the train home, and then studying until 11:00pm. On weekends, I slept "late" until 6:00am and then studied until at least 9:00pm, with just a short break for a run in Prospect Park. It was tedious and monotonous, but exam day finally arrived.

Once the exams concluded, we were able to check our answers against a key. I remember my hands trembling. The good news was that I performed very well. The bad news was also that I performed very well. I realized I would need to maintain this level of scholarship if I were to be accepted into my residency of choice, which was dermatology at the time—one of the most competitive.

In addition to the academic rigor, I found loneliness to be a challenge. Although I had excelled scholastically in college, it would have been a surprise to an outside observer, as I had an extremely active social life. That social life evaporated in medical school, and I missed the camaraderie of friendship.

I also faced another practical challenge. While I was committed to developing a career as a physician, I was simultaneously pursuing an enthusiastic interest in spirituality and philosophy in my "off hours." Juggling both was exhausting.

Midway through the first year, while preparing for my second round of exams, I hit a low point when a long-term romantic relationship ended. I walked home from the subway, feeling despondent. As I turned the corner from Eighth Avenue to President Street and approached my apartment on a downhill stretch, tears filled my eyes. I noticed a stooped-over old man, struggling to walk up the hill. Every step seemed risky. Yet he teetered on, barely steadying himself with his cane. Despite the intense focus he had on keeping his footing, he somehow saw me coming. He even managed to detect my emotional state. As we approached, he stopped and looked up at me. When I drew close enough, he smiled warmly, pleasantly uttered a single phrase, and moved cheerfully on. What he said was something like, "Sometimes, it's hard, but you just have to keep on going." Beyond his age, this strange man looked weathered by experience. I could tell that he had known suffering. Yet he seemed happy. I could also tell that he recognized I was suffering and sincerely wanted me to overcome it. This gave his advice power. It reverberated through me, completely changing my perspective.

I smiled as I entered my apartment, carrying a new sense of hope. I realized that, I too, would make it up the hill as long as I kept going—and that I needed to find a way to be happier along the way. That day marked a shift in how I approached medical school. I resolved to never study the day before a battery of exams. Instead, I would prepare intensively in advance, reserving the day for reading about spirituality and philosophy, as well as exercising. I would also end the day with a celebratory dinner and beer at my favorite restaurant, where I would quietly express kindness and optimism to others. All this change was inspired by a stranger who knew how to deeply care.

ON THE ELIXIR OF LIFE: TRANSFORMATIONAL CARE

I included this example of Transformational Care for several reasons. First, it highlights that even small acts of caring can have a tremendous impact. Second, it illustrates that perfect strangers can provide meaningful care. Third, it shows that it can only take seconds. Fourth, it demonstrates that caregivers often don't know they have made a difference. Lastly, it exemplifies that knowing a difference was made isn't usually the point.

Let's now revisit the story of the Master Alchemist. The tale has little to say about the Elixir of Life in terms of the number of words dedicated to describing it (only

15). However, the description indicates that it's exceedingly potent.

She claimed that in its pure form, it was the most powerful substance on earth.

In chapter 3, I suggested that the Elixir of Life represents what I call Transformational Care, and I clarified that this isn't casual care. It is care delivered with so much intensity that it can cause transformation. The rest of this chapter will more substantively examine Transformational Care.

CARE IS A PROFESSIONAL OBLIGATION BUT NOT AN EMOTIONAL OBLIGATION

When I ask people to perform the allegorical analysis exercise, one of the most common responses is that the Elixir of Life represents love. This is probably because most people believe love is the most powerful non-physical force on earth. Indeed, across time, culture, race, and religion, love is widely recognized as having the highest value, providing the greatest meaning, and being the strongest motivator of behavior.

Despite this relatively universal recognition, the word "love" is uncommonly used in professional circles. There are several reasons for this. First, love is a semantically charged word that can connote romantic or sexual intimacy. Second, love can imply partiality or bias. Third, love can infer dependency. Fourth, love is difficult to objectively define and measure. Fifth, love can involve impulsiveness, irrationality, and infatuation. Lastly (and related to these other reasons), Western culture has traditionally relegated love to the personal sector.

Alternatively, the word "care" captures the pertinent elements of the word love, without the aspects that can be professionally inappropriate. Care allows for concern, attentiveness, support, and responsibility, without implying romantic or sexual intimacy. Care can be distributed fairly and equally, without favoritism. Care avoids dependency by promoting empowerment, independence, and agency. Care can be defined and measured in terms of duties, standards, and practices. Care allows for empathy and compassion, with appropriate emotional restraint and boundaries. Lastly, care is consistent with Western professional ethics and norms. This makes the word care an excellent choice for what the Elixir of Life represents in the professional setting.

The best professional organizations believe that leaders have an unequivocal duty to care for employees. This obligation arises from the power and responsibility bestowed upon them. Where power and responsibility exist, care is required to prevent harm, promote well-being, support dignity, and inform ethical decision making.[6,15,16]

Conversely, most organizations believe that leaders are not absolutely required to have fondness for, feel emotional affection toward, be friends with, or provide emotional fulfillment to employees. This distinguishes the professional obligation to care from an emotional one.[15,16]

Research has clearly demonstrated that leadership care can confer significant competitive advantage by improving organizational culture, organizational citizenship, engagement, retention, teamwork, innovation, and performance. Studies have also shown that not all leadership care is equally effective. The most impactful forms of care are ethical and principled, structural and systemic, and clearly connected to organizational strategy. They support individual well-being, promote individual empowerment and autonomy, and create psychological safety.[15,16,17,18,19]

While utilizing leadership care in these ways may seem like common sense, a 2024 Deloitte survey identified a dramatic perception gap, where 75 percent of managers believed they made employee well-being a priority, but only 54 percent of employees perceived this to be the case.[20] Gallup survey data from 2024 corroborated this, indicating that only 39 percent of US workers strongly agreed that their manager cared about them as a person, a decline from 47 percent in 2020.[21] Clearly, the average manager has opportunity to better express their care.

Transformational Care Requires Caring Leadership

For care to be transformational, it must be authentically felt. This is an intrinsic requirement of leaders that has profound ramifications for themselves and their employees.

There are two primary ways that authentic care can go wrong. The first is when a leader either cares only minimally or doesn't care at all. This can be due to institutional forces that discourage care. Some examples include structures that foster dehumanization or emotional distance, professional norms that encourage unhealthy competition or fear, and incentives that reward output at the expense of people.[20,22]

Belief and value conflicts can also create situations where a leader thinks they should not care. These can include cultures that discourage the display of warmth, that encourage a transactional vs. relational work philosophy, and that espouse an authoritarian vs. collaborative approach to workplace relationships.[22,23]

A leader may also simply not know how to care because of skill or development gaps. This may stem from a lack of role models who expressed care, underdeveloped emotional intelligence, or a lack of practice.[30,24]

Finally, personal capacity may be the limiting factor. Certain environmental constraints can contribute to this, including stress and overload, time pressure, crisis, burnout, and compassion fatigue. Personality traits and relational patterns can also constrain the capacity for caring, including maladaptive perfectionism, a high dominance / low agreeableness orientation, an avoidant attachment orientation, narcissism, and Machiavellianism. Each of these dynamics can range from mild to severe, collectively reducing a leader's capacity for authentic care to varying degrees.[22,25,26,27,28,29,30,31]

The second way that authentic care can go wrong is when it is performative rather than genuine. Many of the factors previously discussed can predispose a leader to such inauthenticity. Leaders may act on this predisposition because performative care appears cheaper (requiring less investment), safer (entailing less vulnerability), and easier to advertise (attracting greater reward).[22,23,24,25,27,28,29]

The consequences of a lack of care in the work environment are obvious, and we won't cover them. Instead, we'll focus on the consequences of inauthentic, performative care.

Inauthentic care may be subtler than an absolute lack of care, but it's still extremely detrimental. For leaders, the cognitive dissonance involved in managing a discrepancy between expressed and actual sentiment creates long-term emotional strain that can manifest as guilt, anxiety, and burnout. Inauthentic care can also impair decision quality through the distraction of having to maintain the façade. Emotionally intelligent employees can usually detect the hypocrisy, resulting in an erosion of leader credibility, influence, and authority. For employees, inauthentic care destroys psychological safety, fosters distrust, creates disengagement, increases stress and burnout, and weakens organizational citizenship. Inauthentic care makes Transformational Care impossible.[30,32,33,34]

On the other hand, authentically felt care is tremendously beneficial to both the leader and the employee. Leaders who authentically care experience several cognitive benefits. Their perspective is enhanced by a greater awareness of employee strengths, weaknesses, challenges, motivations, needs, and morale. Their perception of organizational and interpersonal patterns and trends is sharpened. And they become more centered in ethical reasoning, anchoring to what is fair and reasonable for their employees and the company. These things improve strategic analysis and decision quality.[35,36,37,38]

Leaders who authentically care also experience many emotional benefits. Their empathy and compassion are enhanced. They enjoy greater job satisfaction and fulfillment. Finally, they experience enhanced motivation, drive, and resilience. Most employees can detect the authenticity. This improves leader credibility, trust, influence, and authority, while also increasing employee engagement. Authentically felt care is an absolute requirement for Transformational Care.[34,35,36,37]

For care to be maximally transformational, however, it isn't enough for it to be authentically felt. It must also be actively expressed.

This, too, can go sideways, primarily when care is felt but not expressed. Authentic care that goes unexpressed is detrimental to both leader and employee, though far less so than inauthentic care. For the leader, the internal conflict of feeling care but not expressing it can stifle the cognitive benefits of authentically felt care previously described, impairing strategic analysis and decision quality. Emotionally, withholding care can generate tension, regret, guilt, shame, frustration, and burnout. Behaviorally, it can manifest as awkwardness, subtle emotional distance, or obvious withdrawal. From the employee's perspective, most can detect the discrepancy. At best, this creates confusion. At worst, it produces the consequences of perceived leadership hypocrisy described earlier.[25,36,39]

Actively expressed authentic care is immensely beneficial. For leaders, the active expression amplifies the benefits of authentically felt care. For employees, it isn't until a leader actively expresses care that the employee becomes fully aware of it. The rest of this chapter will focus on how care can be cultivated and practiced.

Cultivating Transformational Care

Fortunately, because we are biologically and psychosocially predisposed to care, caring tends to arise naturally, albeit to varying degrees among individuals. Unfortunately, life circumstances can erode our capacity to care. But regardless of our current condition, care can be cultivated. At one extreme, this can involve nurturing an abundant reservoir of care. At the other, it can require replenishing one that has been severely depleted. In either case, our capacity for caring can be strengthened through practices that enhance personal wellness, empathy, and compassion.

Personal Wellness

The airline industry knows that it's important for a passenger to put on their own oxygen mask before assisting others. The same goes for care. As leaders, we need to ensure that we care for ourselves so that we can be at our best in caring for others. A comprehensive discussion of wellness is beyond the scope of this book. Instead, we'll focus on two basic but essential practices.

- Practice self-care:

    Self-care is the intentional practice of optimizing your physical, mental, and emotional well-being so you can effectively manage stress and gracefully navigate daily life. This requires meeting the physiological needs of getting adequate sleep, eating nourishing foods, staying hydrated, exercising regularly, avoiding unhealthy habits, and receiving medical care. It can also entail spending time at leisure, staying socially connected, practicing mindfulness or meditation, engaging in religious or spiritual practice, and seeking meaning and fulfillment. Finally, it involves maintaining healthy boundaries, maintaining a healthy work-life balance, and sustaining a dedication to continual self-development.[20,25,26]

While some of these practices may come naturally to you, others may be challenging. Many high-performing leaders, for example, struggle to get adequate sleep and maintain a healthy work-life balance.[20]

- Build personal emotional competence:

Personal emotional competence requires emotional intelligence (EQ), particularly the components of self-awareness and self-management. In *Emotional Intelligence 2.0*, authors Bradberry and Greaves define self-awareness as "your ability to accurately perceive your own emotions in the moment and understand your tendencies across situations."[39] They define self-management as "your ability to use self-awareness of your emotions to stay flexible and direct your behavior positively."[39] Unlike IQ, which is considered fixed, EQ can be enhanced. The art and science of developing EQ is so vital that it is the focus of another book I'm writing, *Blue Water Leadership: Using Emotional Intelligence to Navigate Rough Waters.*

One effective approach to developing self-awareness and self-management involves a structured approach described by the acronym NURSE DARE. The NURSE component focuses on self-awareness, while DARE pertains to self-management. The NURSE framework was originally developed by VitalTalk, a non-profit organization focused on improving clinician-patient communication.[40] It was based on the field of therapeutic communication, which was popularized by Florence Nightingale.[41] I was introduced to the technique during my clinical practice and later adapted it for the purpose of practicing self-awareness, adding the DARE portion for self-management.

The letters in my version of NURSE stand for: *name* the emotion; *understand* why you feel the emotion; *reflect* on the important lesson the emotion provides; *support* yourself during the process; and *evaluate* your options. This is designed to support self-awareness. The letters in DARE stand for: *decide* what to do; *act* on your decision; *review* the consequences; and *explain* the situation to a trusted colleague. This is meant to support self-management.

When emotions are complex and intense, even leaders with high EQ can struggle to respond constructively. And when emotions are straightforward and mild, personal emotional competence can still be refined. In either case, using a structured approach like NURSE DARE can be quite helpful.

In the absence of self-care and personal emotional competence, a leader may be so thirsty for self-refreshment that they are unable to think of assisting others. Conversely, when a leader has a wellspring of personal wellness, their attention will naturally shift outward. Australian author Beau Taplin articulated this beautifully when he said, "Self-love is an ocean, and your heart is a vessel. Make it full, and any excess will spill over into the lives of the people you hold dear." This overflowing begins with empathy and compassion and, when fully expressed, culminates in altruism.

EMPATHY, COMPASSION, AND ALTRUISM

Empathy, compassion, and altruism are personal attributes that exist along a continuum of care, each having distinct features. Empathy involves understanding and resonating with another's emotions. Compassion adds concern and a desire to help. Altruism extends empathy and compassion into action, encompassing behavior intended to benefit another person. Put simply, empathy understands, compassion cares, and altruism gives. All are critical components of Transformational Care, with empathy facilitating compassion, and compassion motivating altruistic action. All can be cultivated.

Because empathy requires both understanding and resonating with another's emotions, developing it requires refining the cognitive skill to comprehend someone else's emotional perspective as well as the emotional ability to attune with it.

The following are some approaches you can use to refine the cognitive skill of empathically understanding another's emotions.

- Develop fluency in your own emotions:

    This requires establishing a sophisticated vocabulary for accurately naming the core and nuanced emotions you experience. Such fluency with your own emotions will allow you to better recognize them in others.

- Practice active listening:

    This entails listening intently, suspending your own internal dialogue, repeating what you have heard, and asking open-ended questions to clarify thoughts and feelings.

- Employ perspective-taking:

    This encompasses imagining a situation from another's viewpoint by considering their background, experiences, abilities, and constraints.

- Observe and interpret emotional cues:

    This relates to noticing non-verbal signals (body language, facial expressions, and speech qualities) and linking them to potential emotions.

- Avoid judgment:

    This involves suspending personal prejudices that might otherwise impair perception.

- Solicit feedback:

    This calls for transparently and humbly validating your observations by asking the other person if they are accurate.

- Avoid emotional contagion:

  This necessitates having emotional boundaries by being able to feel another's emotions without taking them on. This is somewhat akin to wine tasting: you look at, smell, and taste the wine, but then spit it out. This approach allows you to appreciate the unique qualities of several wines without being under the influence.

Developing an advanced cognitive ability to understand another's emotions paves the way to achieving greater emotional resonance. Here are some methods of nurturing the emotional resonance component of empathy.

- Develop comfort with your own emotions:

  This involves becoming personally comfortable with unpleasant emotions like sadness, fear, and anger, so you aren't prone to repression, suppression, or denial when you encounter them in others.

- Have emotional presence:

  This requires suspending your own thoughts and feelings and allowing yourself to feel the emotions the other person is feeling. Of note, this changes in the compassion phase (to be discussed shortly).

- Utilize validation:

  This entails making constructive comments that support the other person's emotional state based on your understanding of their situation and perspective.

- Avoid empathic distress:

  This necessitates having emotional boundaries by remaining in a supportive role rather than assuming responsibility. It can also require limiting exposure when necessary.

It's important to remember that empathy should involve not only sharing in the unpleasant emotions that others feel, but also in their pleasant ones. A caring leader participates in both the troubles and the triumphs of those they lead.

When you feel emotions strongly, empathy is a powerful precursor to compassion, often being all that's necessary to motivate the desire to help. However, because compassion involves your own emotional response rather than mirroring another's, practicing it requires a unique skillset. Here are some ways you can cultivate compassion.

- Adopt a servant leader mindset and heart-set:

  This encompasses believing that helping others is a moral and ethical imperative, as well as a professional responsibility.

- Pay it forward:

  This entails appreciating the assistance you have personally received and reciprocating by helping others.

- Adopt a compassionate pedagogy:

  This requires putting your philosophical dedication to compassion into practice by actively exploring opportunities to have compassion for others.

- Avoid compassion fatigue:

  This necessitates avoiding emotional contagion and empathic distress as previously described. It also involves deliberately shifting from empathy to compassion by detaching from the emotions of others and embracing your own emotional stance. In other words, you feel *with* others in empathy, but you feel *about* others in compassion. Furthermore, it requires practicing radical acceptance (described next) and distinguishing between empowering support and disempowering rescue (covered shortly).

- Practice radical acceptance:

  This includes accepting that challenges, struggles, and failures are normal, and success often requires setbacks and temporary suffering. Practicing radical acceptance facilitates the avoidance of disempowering rescue (discussed next).

- Distinguish between empowering support and disempowering rescue:

  This calls for understanding that empowering support involves interventions that preserve autonomy and facilitate self-efficacy, whereas disempowering rescue involves intercessions that violate autonomy and erode self-efficacy. Simply put, empowering support is helping someone to help themselves while disempowering rescue is doing it for them. Although rescue can be appropriate in emergent, high-stakes scenarios, it's usually counterproductive. Many leaders struggle with this distinction and are prone to disempowering rescue.

Altruism tends to be the natural result of empathy and compassion. Given that it requires action, however, we will address it in the next section which moves from the cultivation of Transformational Care to its practice.

To illustrate these concepts, it's my pleasure to introduce you to Maya Hernandez, the first of three hypothetical leaders whose leadership journey we will follow. In this chapter we will read about Maya's journey in three parts. In the next two chapters we'll do the same for Trevon Brooks and Dr. Grace Chen. After reading each scenario, I encourage you to consider how well the leader handled the situation and what insights you can take away for your own leadership.

The Leadership Journey of Maya Hernandez: Part One

Maya Hernandez was a Senior Operations Manager at a rapidly growing logistics technology company. After a brutally challenging year, marked by massive expansion and relentless after-hours crises, she was exhausted. She was running on little sleep, skipping morning workouts, eating poorly, and sacrificing personal and family time. Maya had the self-awareness to recognize that physical and emotional depletion were undermining her ability to lead and support her team. She also realized that her usual calm demeanor had deteriorated, and she had become irritable and impatient. Maya knew she needed to replenish her own emotional reserves.

Maya recommitted to self-care, ensuring that she started the day at the gym and ended it with deep breathing before falling asleep at a reasonable hour. She also made time for yoga classes and family movie nights. She established a deliberate practice of using emotional intelligence to identify stress in the moment and manage it constructively. From this steadier internal state, she was able to extend empathy and compassion to others. She actively listened to concerns, noted subtle emotional cues, maintained emotional presence, and validated feelings without unnecessary emotional absorption. She embraced her servant-leader mindset, offering support when her influence was needed, while empowering her team to overcome other challenges independently—all in ways that were sustainable and avoided compassion fatigue.

Over time, Maya became increasingly emotionally present and composed during high-pressure situations. Her team responded by deepening their trust and strengthening their commitment to excellence. The division was eventually recognized for both superior culture and performance. Maya had come to understand that her capacity to care for others would be either constrained or enhanced by her ability to care for herself.

Finding the Elixir of Life: Practicing Transformational Care

Mastering the art of driving change through the active application of Transformational Care requires the development of foundational aptitude and continual practice. Now that we've covered aptitude, here are some approaches you can use to enhance your delivery of Transformational Care, beginning with altruistic intervention.

Altruistic Intervention

Altruism refers to intentional, voluntary actions taken to improve welfare or alleviate distress, without expecting an external reward. Before we address intentionality and volunteerism, let's focus on relinquishing the desire for reward.

At the extremes, the difference between selfless and selfish giving is obvious to both the giver and the receiver. In subtle cases, however, what can sometimes complicate the distinction is the fact that altruism feels good. There's no avoiding this, as altruistic acts trigger the reflex release of neurochemicals like oxytocin, dopamine, and endorphins, that reduce stress and increase happiness. The litmus test for altruism, therefore, can't be whether there is personal benefit to the act of giving—because there always will be. The differentiator must be intention.

If the assistance was provided because the giver wanted to experience something positive in return, this does not qualify as true altruism. This disqualification doesn't nullify the fact that assistance was rendered, but it does mean it wasn't truly altruistic. This kind of giving is often called transactional service or social exchange. However, if the assistance was provided purely because empathy and compassion encouraged it, and the giver experienced the good feeling as a side effect, it qualifies as altruism.[29,39]

This distinction raises some interesting questions, unique to the professional sphere. Given that leaders have a fiduciary responsibility to drive organizational success and that altruism requires a leader to have no expectation of external reward, is it philosophically *inappropriate* and practically *unreasonable* for a leader to strive to practice altruism in the workplace? After all, lack of desire and effort to achieve organizational success, as well as lack of results in achieving it, are all indisputable forms of leadership failure. Consequently, should a leader adopt the practice of transactional service instead of altruism? My answer is a resounding no.

The benchmark here, again, is a matter of intent. If a leader intends the reward to benefit the organization and not themselves, this simultaneously meets the qualifications for altruism and fulfills a leader's fiduciary responsibilities.

Between these extremes is a gray area, as it's possible for a leader to intend to direct the reward to both the organization and to themselves. This can be done in obvious or surreptitious ways. Regardless, I have found that there is a strong correlation between the purity of a leader's altruistic intent and the efficacy of their leadership care. Furthermore, I believe that the relationship is causal. Therefore, to the degree that a leader cares for and unselfishly gives of themselves to their employees, those employees will tend to care for and unselfishly give to the company. This fact is the driving force for why selfless Transformational Care not only changes individuals but also changes organizations.

Now that we've established that altruism is philosophically appropriate, practically reasonable, and highly effectual, we will shift to its practice. The following are some strategies you can employ to enhance your practice of altruism.

- Create a culture of care and psychological safety:

  When you create a culture that prioritizes well-being, empathy, compassion, and mutual support, employees feel known, respected, valued, and cared for as individuals. This foundation of care fosters psychological safety, empowering them to speak openly, admit uncertainty, take risks, and learn from mistakes without fear of reprisal.[19,28]

- Strive for cumulative continuity:

  In the *Tao Te Ching*, Lao Tzu says that "Great acts are made up of small deeds."[42] This holds for altruism, especially in the context of Leadership Alchemy. The practice of continuously identifying small opportunities to provide altruistic intervention allows you to have a tremendously positive impact over time. This is also a more approachable task than trying to eat the altruism elephant all at once.

- Look for ways to both provide benefit and reduce hassle:

  It can be useful to divide your search for altruistic opportunities into the broad categories of providing benefit and reducing hassle. Providing benefit involves interventions that improve the situation by adding something good. Reducing hassle involves interventions that improve the situation by removing something bad.

  In a series of studies from 2020-2025, Junca Silva and colleagues concluded that daily hassles, defined as minor but frequent negative micro-events, were more detrimental to employee well-being than major, isolated life events.[43] This was due to their cumulative impact. Clearly, there's an altruistic opportunity to deliver Transformational Care by reducing hassles.

- Practice principled altruism:

  You can cultivate true altruism in several ways. These include improving personal wellness, building empathy and compassion, making altruism a core value, strengthening self-esteem, practicing giving without seeking recognition, learning from altruistic role models, and shifting from a focus on self to a focus on others.[30,39]

  A useful exercise in shifting the focus to others is to spend time avoiding statements that use the words "I, me, my, or mine." Fair warning: this can be awkward in the professional setting and may be best practiced with people outside of work.

- Maintain fairness and justice:

  Even well-intentioned leaders can cause harm when fairness or justice is compromised. Unfairness may occur through favoritism, inconsistent expectations, selective recognition, or uneven access to opportunities. Injustice can emerge when leaders maintain policies that disadvantage some individuals, tolerate misconduct, or fail to address power imbalances.[6,18,22,34]

  These failures often arise unintentionally through unconscious bias and can manifest in subtle ways. Through dedicated self-awareness and self-management, leaders can act more consistently and judiciously, fostering an environment of trust, psychological safety, and belonging.[22,34]

Transparent Communication

Demonstrating care through altruistic intervention is essential, as caring words without caring deeds lack credibility. At the same time, it's equally important to transparently communicate that you care, as caring deeds without caring words can seem impersonal. Therefore, you should be intentional about conveying care through both non-verbal and verbal modalities.

Some approaches that you can utilize to non-verbally communicate care are as follows.

- Body language:

  You can communicate care by assuming an open posture with uncrossed arms and relaxed shoulders, fully facing the person, and leaning slightly toward them while seated.

- Facial expression:

  You can demonstrate care through soft and responsive facial expressions, genuine smiles when appropriate, and concerned expressions when called for. It's also important to avoid stiff or off-putting expressions.

- Eye behavior:

  You can convey care through comfortable eye contact (not staring). You should also avoid looking elsewhere (e.g., at a cell phone).

- Paralanguage:

  Care can be imparted with a warm tone, moderate pace, appropriate titration of volume (softer for sensitive topics and louder for mutually exciting topics), and pauses that allow others to process the conversation.

- Appearance and artifacts:

  Care can be shown through appropriate and respectful attire and accessories, personal grooming, clean and organized environments, and the thoughtful use of shared tools.

- Use of space:

  Care can be transmitted through appropriate distancing that respects personal boundaries by never becoming too close, as well as by calibrating the distance to reflect the nature of the interaction (closer for support and farther for formality). Sitting or standing at the same level also expresses care.

- Appropriate touch:

  You can communicate care through professionally appropriate touch (a handshake, a high-five, a fist bump, a supportive hand on the shoulder), as well avoidance of touch when receptivity is uncertain.

- Use of time:

  You can demonstrate care by making time for meaningful connection, listening to others with full attention (without interruption or distraction), not rushing conversations, being punctual, and meeting deadlines. Making time for meaningful connection tends to be a major area of opportunity.

It is important for a leader to be aware of how well they communicate care through these non-verbal modalities. You can assess the first five by recording a video of yourself during a meeting (with the consent of the participants). You can evaluate the rest through a combination of self-reflection and feedback from trusted colleagues. Becoming adept at naturally communicating care in these ways is an extremely impactful and underappreciated way of delivering Transformational Care. This is largely because the constancy of non-verbal communication allows you to establish an aura of caring in an unassuming way. When done effectively, people will feel cared about without you ever telling them.

Coupling these non-verbal approaches with the verbal communication of care, however, is essential. Here are some verbal techniques for communicating care.

- Tell employees that you care about their professional well-being:

  While it may seem obvious, some leaders don't do this at all, and others do it seldomly. A statement that can be universally applicable is, "I care about creating an environment where you enjoy the work you're doing and the people you're doing it with." You can also make comments of care about the employee's professional development and goals, such as, "I care about helping you to develop and meet your professional goals."

  In all cases, it's important that your expressions are genuine, not overdone, well-timed, delivered in the appropriate setting, consistent with non-verbal signals, and reinforced with caring behaviors.

- Provide recognition:

  This can include statements of praise for performance, appreciation for effort (apart from performance), and celebration of personal and professional milestones (birthdays and work anniversaries). Recognition is most impactful when it is timely, credible, specific, and reinforced by behavior. Credibility is built by consistently demonstrating care, fulfilling commitments related to care, and being transparent about limitations. Specificity is related to your care being objectively observable. It is created by referencing concrete events, highlighting the impact, and using quantitative measures. Behavioral reinforcement involves accompanying words with actions. This can be accomplished by following your comments with tangible support or rewards and aligning verbal and non-verbal signals of care.[16,20,21]

Finally, it's important to recognize both individuals and teams. Individual recognition is most appropriate when the contribution was distinct, visible, and personally owned. Team recognition is most appropriate when the contribution was interdependent and collective.[16,21]

- Celebrate success:

Recognition and celebration are closely related but serve distinct purposes. Recognition centers on effort and achievement, reinforcing motivation through frequent, ongoing acknowledgment. Celebration, in contrast, focuses on milestones and meaning, periodically bringing people together to build collective pride. Both are essential, as recognition without celebration can leave teams feeling appreciated but depleted, while celebration without recognition can cause individuals to feel unseen. Using them together over time strengthens individuals, teams, performance, and culture.[16,21,39]

- Provide support and encouragement during times of struggle and disappointment:

This can include acknowledging the reality of the struggle or disappointment, being present and not evaluative, validating appropriate emotional responses, and separating employee worth and effort from outcome. It can also involve reflecting on the value of lessons learned, recalling how prior setbacks were eventually overcome, highlighting potential next steps, offering assistance, and closing with an endorsement of confidence while avoiding undue pressure.

- Tell employees that you care about their personal well-being:

Personal care and professional care are distinct. Generally, employees feel more cared for when leaders express care for them as people, not just as professionals.[16,41]

Expressions of personal care are most powerful when they are observant, tied to well-being vs. performance, respectful of boundaries, and use empathetic language. Observant expressions of care involve things that require attention to detect, such as when an employee has experienced stress outside of work (e.g., caring for a sick parent). Focusing on well-being requires prioritizing the person over their performance by showing care for how they feel about certain events, milestones, aspirations, and concerns. Respecting boundaries involves limiting your comments to comfortable topics, avoiding intrusion, and using open-ended questions. Using empathetic language focuses on active listening, acknowledging feelings, and validating experiences.[16,41]

While it's stating the obvious, these non-verbal and verbal expressions of care require meaningful interaction between the leader and the employee. In the high-paced, high-stakes, results-oriented, and often virtual environment characteristic of many businesses, creating the time and space for such meaningful interactions can be difficult. This was mentioned in the section on use of time and tends to be one of the biggest areas of opportunity for leaders.[20,21]

The Leadership Journey of Maya Hernandez: Part Two

Several years later, Maya had accepted a position as the Product Director for a mid-sized healthcare software company. She was leading a high-performing team through a critical platform update, encumbered by a tight timeline and significant organizational scrutiny. While the team trusted her immensely, they were intimidated by the complexity and importance of the project. Several also felt that "corporate" didn't fully understand the demands placed upon them or appreciate their efforts. Drawing on earlier lessons, Maya knew that maintaining internal steadiness was critical. But she also recognized that it wouldn't be enough. She would need to be highly intentional in expressing care outwardly.

She systematically looked for ways to demonstrate care through action—adding resources, postponing lower-priority projects, redistributing work, removing barriers, and cancelling non-critical meetings. In daily interactions, she used calm posture, warm eye contact, a reassuring tone, and focused attention to signal availability and respect. She explicitly acknowledged the stress the team was under, stated her commitment to supporting their professional and personal well-being, and expressed confidence in their ability to succeed. She recognized effort, celebrated wins, validated frustrations without minimizing them, and expressed optimism about the future.

Within weeks, the team became more confident and energized. Emotional defensiveness eased, progress accelerated, and the update was successful. The CEO hosted a dinner at her home, personally thanked everyone, and presented the team with an award of excellence. She later told Maya that she wanted to discuss opportunities for further advancement, noting Maya's ability to lead through demanding circumstances by creating a culture of care.

Humble Receptivity

Care is not a one-way street. So far, we've focused on how a leader can deliver care through expressive behavior. Practicing care through receptive behavior is equally important and can be done in several ways, all marked by humble receptivity. You can cultivate humble receptivity by adopting the following practices.

- Make it more important to *get it right* than to *be right*:

    Humility is an exacting virtue in that when you think you have it, you have often lost it. T.S. Elliot addressed this paradox poetically when he said, "The only wisdom we can hope to acquire is the wisdom of humility." Adopting an attitude where you care far more about getting it right than being right sets the stage for humble receptivity, because it prioritizes the truth while neutralizing arrogance, conceit, and defensiveness.

- Have an open-door policy:

    Having an open-door policy increases accessibility and encourages feedback. It's critical to note that it is only effective when there's enough psychological safety for employees to walk through the door.

- Seek feedback:

    Beyond having an open-door policy where employees can come to you at their discretion, you should actively solicit feedback from employees on the other side of the doorway. This can be feedback about their overall work experience, policies, processes, company goals, and incentives. It can also be feedback about your leadership.

- Accept and value feedback:

  The ancient Roman historian Cornelius Tacitus said, "Fear is not in the habit of speaking truth; when perfect sincerity is expected, perfect freedom must be allowed." When asking for feedback, you must be prepared to hear difficult things. Regardless of how repugnant the feedback is, if it's given respectfully and appropriately, it should be received the same way. Furthermore, the candor should be rewarded.

  When the feedback is hard to hear, you should judiciously evaluate its validity. It can be helpful to consider that a feeling of "I resent that feedback" can sometimes mean "I resemble that feedback." In other words, an intense emotional response can signal that there's truth to it. Rather than getting defensive, get curious. Asking clarifying questions and seeking additional feedback from trusted employees or colleagues can be invaluable.

  Some leaders have just as much, or even more, trouble accepting positive feedback or praise that is altruistically given. If (like me) you're one of these leaders, you should note that graciously accepting it can have an incredibly positive impact on your employees.

- Be vulnerable:

  This involves acknowledging errors without defensiveness, apologizing without qualification, admitting uncertainty, appropriately disclosing thoughts and feelings, appropriately divulging growth areas and struggles, and sharing relevant purpose-driven personal stories.

Being vulnerable can be uncomfortable for a multitude of reasons, including fear of appearing incapable, fear of eroding respect, fear of reprisal, and exacerbation of imposter syndrome. However, vulnerability increases psychological safety, increases trust, enhances belonging, reduces burnout, fosters teamwork, encourages creativity and innovation, and speeds up problem-solving. It also increases leader credibility, authority, and influence.[34,35,36,37]

The Leadership Journey of Maya Hernandez: Part Three

Following her success as a Product Director, Maya was promoted to Vice President of Operations at the same rapidly developing healthcare software company. She inherited a cross-functional team responsible for platform reliability, regulatory readiness, and customer escalations. While performance metrics appeared acceptable, Maya quickly sensed deeper problems. Her predecessor had driven results through intimidation, and team members had learned to stay quiet, rather than surface concerns. Serious software defects, validation gaps, and potential compliance risks were going unreported, creating hidden exposure in a highly regulated environment.

Maya understood that restoring transparency would require humble receptivity at the leadership level. She held a mandatory town hall, expressed her commitment to collaboration and psychological safety, and openly acknowledged that she couldn't succeed without honest input. She committed to weekly meetings with functional leaders, monthly open forums for broader teams, and an open-door policy. She promised to listen and make changes based on what she was told. She followed through by visibly acting on feedback, publicly crediting ideas from others, and admitting when she had missed something herself. By modeling vulnerability, she reinforced that it was more important for the organization to get it right than for her to be right.

As psychological safety increased, team members began surfacing concerns earlier, sharing lessons learned, and collaborating across silos. The organization shifted from guarded compliance to shared ownership. Maya's willingness to humbly listen, learn, and be vulnerable proved to be a major driver of organizational success.

Chapter Summary

We began this chapter by recalling the Master Alchemist's description of the Elixir of Life: *She claimed that in its pure form, it was the most powerful substance on earth.* We revisited my suggestion that it represented Transformational Care, and my clarification that it isn't casual care. It is care, so intense, so fully given, that it can spark a transformation.

We then established that for care to be transformational, it must be both authentically felt and actively expressed. We described how authentic care can be cultivated through personal wellness, empathy, and compassion. Numerous practices were described and are outlined here:

Personal Wellness

- Practice self-care
- Build personal emotional competence

Empathy

- Develop fluency in your own emotions
- Practice active listening
- Employ perspective-taking
- Observe and interpret emotional cues
- Avoid judgment
- Solicit feedback
- Avoid emotional contagion
- Develop comfort with your own emotions
- Have emotional presence
- Utilize validation
- Avoid empathic distress

Compassion

- Adopt a servant leader mindset and heart-set
- Pay it forward
- Adopt a compassionate pedagogy
- Avoid compassion fatigue
- Practice radical acceptance
- Distinguish between empowering support and dis-empowering rescue

Finally, we discussed how you can practice Transformational Care through altruistic intervention, transparent non-verbal and verbal communication, and humble receptivity. Various techniques were described and are summarized here:

Altruistic Intervention

- Create a culture of care and psychological safety
- Strive for cumulative continuity
- Look for ways to both provide benefit and reduce hassle
- Practice principled altruism
- Maintain fairness and justice

Transparent Non-verbal Communication of Care

- Body language
- Facial expression
- Eye behavior
- Paralanguage
- Appearance and artifacts
- Use of space
- Appropriate touch
- Use of time

Transparent Verbal Communication of Care

- Tell employees that you care about their professional well-being
- Provide recognition
- Celebrate success
- Provide support and encouragement during times of struggle and disappointment

- Tell employees that you care about their personal well-being

Humble Receptivity

- Make it more important to get it right than to be right
- Have an open-door policy
- Seek feedback
- Accept and value feedback
- Be vulnerable

These approaches to cultivating and practicing Transformational Care are both practical and powerful. If you use them regularly, you will find yourself in possession of an Elixir of Life that can be used to bring about meaningful change in individuals and organizations.

8

THE PHILOSOPHER'S STONE: DELIVERING TRANSFORMATIONAL CHALLENGE

Regarding the Philosopher's Stone. . .

She claimed that it had to be able to cause a powerful reaction.

Mrs. Swenson

Having been a voracious reader and aspiring poet from an early age, I entered high school convinced I was an advanced writer. Then I met Mrs. Swenson, my tenth grade English teacher. Mrs. Swenson was a no-nonsense woman of wisdom and paradox. She was fiercely intense about the pursuit of excellence, but just as lighthearted about the journey. She also had a passion for truth and an irreverent disregard for convention. I found her simultaneously intriguing and intimidating.

She taught in the Socratic style, and by the end of the first month, I believed I had made several impressive contributions. I had also earned high scores on our initial exams. When it came time to submit our first essay, I was excited to get feedback. She had us alphabetically file to the front of the room and distributed our papers, bombastically announcing our first names followed by our grades: "Anne—B-plus, Danny—C, Frank—B," and so on. When it was my turn, she snarled, "Michael—F. See me after class." She accompanied it with a mischievous smile, but I could tell she was serious. I was mortified. When we spoke after class, the conversation went something like this:

Mrs. Swenson: So, what do you think F stands for?

Michael: Maybe fantastic?

Mrs. Swenson: No. Try again.

Michael: Maybe fabulous?

*Mrs. Swenson: F stands for f**king terrible. Figure out what you did wrong and then do it again.*

Michael: I thought it was good. Can I get a hint?

Mrs. Swenson: Your writing is flowery and indulgent. Your sentences have too many commas, semicolons, parentheses, and dashes. I can't stand reading them. You're missing the point of why we write. Do it over. I want it tomorrow.

Michael: OK.

My favorite author at that time was JRR Tolkien. I found his writing beautiful, and his storytelling enchanting. I had adopted much of his style, including vivid sensory descriptions, inversions of subjects and verbs, the linking of many different concepts through stacked conjunctions, and the liberal use of commas, semicolons, dashes, and parentheses. Mrs. Swenson didn't appreciate this. I rewrote and resubmitted the essay. I thought it was much better. Mrs. Swenson did not. She read it in front of me, chuckled, and wrote a giant red D on it.

Mrs. Swenson: Let's try this again. What do you think D stands for?

Michael: Maybe delightful?

*Mrs. Swenson: No. D stands for do it f**king again. It's still too much about you and not enough about the reader. Writing should never be about you.*

I was speechless—this time, not because I was mortified. I grasped what she said and knew she was right. Until then, I had written mainly for the joy of creativity. I had made it about me, never critically evaluating the merit (or lack thereof) of this approach. Suddenly, there was much to consider. I rewrote the essay. When I handed it in, I was nervous. Like the day before, she read it in front of me. When she finished, she took off her glasses, smiled pleasantly, wrote a B on it, and handed it back.

Mrs. Swenson: B is for better. Now you're starting to get it.

Michael: Thank you for helping me.

Mrs. Swenson: I'm not done.

We engaged in a series of exchanges about my writing throughout the year. Her critiques only became more direct and demanding. I felt like a piece of metal being shaped by a blacksmith whose furnace was furiously hot, whose hammer was painfully heavy, whose anvil was unforgivingly hard, and whose arm never tired.

Eventually, I earned an A-plus in the class. It wasn't so much that I changed my writing style, though I certainly did. The real change was that my writing became about presenting things to others in a way that served them, not me. Mrs. Swenson was an agent of Transformational Challenge.

PROFESSOR SMITH

While completing my studies at the College of William and Mary, one of the required subjects was English. There were two first-year English courses, one taught by a professor who had a reputation for being brilliant but notoriously challenging.

The first day with this professor was brief. After we took our seats, she slowly and elegantly wrote her name on the chalkboard (yes, we had a chalkboard) and said the following (also slowly and elegantly):

> *My name is Professor Smith. God writes A papers. I write A-minus papers. Y'all are capable of anything less. If you have come to this class to get an A, you have come to the wrong place. If you have come to learn something, I will see you next time. Class dismissed.*

While Professor Smith's reputation had preceded her, I didn't expect that! I was caught between two desires. From a practical standpoint, I wanted to get into medical school, and I had to maximize my GPA. Getting a C could ruin my chances. From an ideological standpoint, I wanted to learn. I decided to get more information.

As the other students left, I approached Professor Smith and transparently explained my predicament. She suggested that I bring three writing samples for review, and she assigned me a short story to read. When I brought the samples to her office, she asked penetrating questions about my interpretation of the story. She provided no feedback and said she would have more to say after reviewing my writing.

I don't remember the subject matter of the next class, but I recall being enthralled. Her reputation for brilliance had been understated. I wanted to stay enrolled. After class, she told me I would have to work extraordinarily hard, but that I might be able to earn a B. In her pleasant southern drawl, she emphasized "extraordinarily" (phonetically reducing it to four syllables, as *ex-tror-din-narly*) and "might" (phonetically endowing it with two syllables, as *my-ight*). She also politely added that my writing samples and story interpretation currently met her standards for C-minus work.

I stayed in the class, and I did work *ex-tror-din-narly* hard. The most common thing she said to me was "go deeper." Even when I came to what I believed was a profound realization, she challenged me to go deeper still. I spent long hours contemplating the literal and symbolic meanings of the various works we studied, and they became a source of great inspiration to me. Ultimately, I got a B-plus in the class. She shook my hand and told me very few students had ever earned that grade, and none any higher. Given that God wrote A papers, and she wrote A-minus papers, I considered my B-plus a major achievement.

ON THE PHILOSOPHER'S STONE: TRANSFORMATIONAL CHALLENGE

It is true that I learned a tremendous amount about literature and writing from these teachers. But I included them as examples of Transformational Challenge because they taught me invaluable lessons about myself and life—lessons that couldn't have been imparted without the intensity of their challenges.

Mrs. Swenson helped me see that the merit of any endeavor isn't in what it can do for me, but rather what it can do for others. She also forced me to let go of personal preferences. Finally, she showed me that intensity is often required to create change, much like the formation of certain precious stones from exposure to heat and pressure.

Professor Smith encouraged me to be courageous in striving for lofty and challenging goals rather than superficial and easier ones. She pushed me to search deeply for wisdom and helped me grasp that elusive truths don't surrender their secrets until they are diligently deserved. Finally, she helped me understand that a hard-earned B-plus in anything is far more valuable than an easy A.

Let's turn our attention back to the story of the Master Alchemist. It has even less to say about the Philosopher's Stone (at only 13 words) than it did for the Elixir of

Life. But the description suggests that it is dynamically catalytic.

> *She claimed that it had to be able to cause a powerful reaction.*

In chapter 3, I suggested that the Philosopher's Stone represents what I call Transformational Challenge, and I clarified that this isn't ordinary challenge. It is challenge, so intensely delivered, that it can trigger a transformation. The rest of this chapter will examine Transformational Challenge in greater detail.

Challenge is a Professional Obligation

The teachers that I featured in this chapter believed it was their job to challenge their students. And when they saw a willing and capable student in me, they heightened their efforts. It's your job as a leader to challenge your employees, especially those with potential. John Quincy Adams put it eloquently when he said, "If your actions inspire others to dream more, learn more, do more, and become more, you are a leader."

Challenging employees can include meeting goals, improving performance and results, refining methods and processes, increasing competencies, and advancing within the organization. Research has shown that appropriately challenging employees improves employee performance and engagement, as well as organizational outcomes.[44,45,46,47]

Transformational Challenge Requires Proactive Leadership

Before a leader can issue a challenge externally, they must recognize the opportunity internally. Effectively doing this at scale requires a shift from reactive management to proactive leadership. Reactive managers operate in firefighting mode, addressing problems after they arise. In this atmosphere of near-constant crisis, there is usually little time and energy left for anything else. Consequently, reactive leaders spend so much time fixing things that they do negligible building. They play mostly defense and minimal offense.

In contrast, proactive leaders operate in a forward-looking, strategically oriented fashion, identifying and addressing potential issues before they develop, and devoting significant time to seeking opportunities for improvement. In this atmosphere of strategic control, there is sufficient bandwidth left for elective activities. Proactive leaders spend less time fixing and more time building; less time defending and more time attacking.

Unfortunately, making this shift is easier said than done. Fortunately, it is possible. The following are some strategies you can use to become a more proactive leader.

- Invest in building exceptionally healthy organizational culture and team dynamics:

  In today's results-oriented environment, within which operational outcomes and processes demand attention, it can be difficult to spend time on anything else. I call this "operational preoccupation."

Operational preoccupation often precludes senior leaders from doing the work of building exceptionally healthy organizational culture and team dynamics. This is exacerbated by the fact that operational outcomes are concrete and easily measured, while organizational culture and team dynamics are abstract and difficult to quantify. Furthermore, while operational investments can be made quickly and yield near-immediate results, investments in culture and team dynamics take time to make and mature.

Despite these challenges, the presence of exceptionally healthy organizational culture and team dynamics has been shown to significantly improve organizational outcomes, as well as employee engagement. It also creates an atmosphere of psychological safety, within which Transformational Challenge is more successful (more on this shortly).[16,17,18]

Finally, I strongly believe that achieving exceptionally healthy organizational culture and team dynamics is one of the most effective ways a leader can create sustainable competitive advantage. Investing in organizational culture and team dynamics should, therefore, be a major leadership imperative.[18,20]

- Encourage constructive conflict:

  Constructive conflict is the open, respectful exchange of differing perspectives and ideas, intended to inform decisions, identify solutions, and drive improvement. You can encourage it by creating psychological safety, soliciting diverse viewpoints, modeling curiosity, and facilitating structured discussions. Handled constructively, such conflict promotes learning and innovation, while enhancing engagement and commitment to shared decisions.[28,46,48]

- Create a strategic plan, disseminate it, and navigate from it:

   Operational preoccupation also frequently results in what I call "strategic autopilot." This can be avoided by developing a strategic plan. The best strategic plans have three levels: a concise list of carefully chosen strategic priorities, concrete strategic objectives for each priority, and accompanying strategic tactics to achieve each objective.[49,50]

   Once developed, the strategic plan should be disseminated to all appropriate parties to ensure alignment. Progress should be tracked, and strategic control should be conducted accordingly. Taking these steps does wonders in facilitating a shift to proactive leadership.

- Refine and hardwire operational processes and tactics:

   The operational processes and tactics central to the business, as outlined in the strategic plan, should be hardwired to the ground level. This allows you to function at a higher level, focusing on where the proverbial trains should be going next, rather than why they are running late.

- Develop sophisticated business analytics and monitor performance in real-time:

What you do not measure, you cannot manage. Developing the capacity to contemporaneously and transparently measure key performance metrics significantly improves management effectiveness and efficiency. This leaves you more time for proactive leadership.

- Protect time for strategic planning and use it to identify defensive issues and offensive opportunities:

Few things are more ephemeral than white space on a business leader's calendar. One solution is to block protected time dedicated to strategic planning. You can then use it to address impending issues before they become the "disaster du jour" and to play offense. Aside from being practical, this is much more fun than firefighting.

- Stop having 60- and 30-minute meetings:

A meeting scheduled for 60 minutes can almost always be accomplished in 45. Similarly, a meeting scheduled for 30 minutes can almost always be completed in 20. This is especially true if you require all meetings to have an agenda which is distributed in advance and assigs an owner for every item. The 15 or 10 minutes saved can be used to address pressing issues that might otherwise pile up. Unnecessary meetings can also be eliminated altogether.

- Develop leaders, empower them, and delegate appropriately:

While this requires significant up-front investment, the long-term return is exponential. Well-developed leaders become stewards of culture, champions of teamwork, and key contributors to strategy. They also take ownership of sustaining and refining core organizational processes, reducing reliance on senior leaders for daily operations. As these leaders become more engaged and replicate this approach with their own teams, leadership capacity scales and the organization is strengthened overall.[6,20]

- Incentivize desired behaviors and outcomes:

    Such incentives should ideally be tied to strategic priorities and objectives and then shared with all relevant stakeholders. These incentives can be structured and formally evaluated at regular intervals, as well as unstructured, informal, and intermittent. They can also be monetary or non-monetary. A combination tends to be optimal.[50,52]

> ## The Leadership Journey of Trevon Brooks: Part One
>
> Trevon Brooks was the local Plant Operations Manager for a national manufacturing company providing industrial equipment. He quickly earned respect for his composure under pressure by responding decisively to the constant crises of equipment failures, supply chain disruptions, staffing shortages, and demand surges. Eventually, however, Trevon realized that perpetual firefighting left little room for process improvement, safety enhancements, or sustainable growth. He knew that maintaining performance at scale would require a fundamental shift from reactive management to proactive leadership.

To initiate this shift, Trevon convened a series of workshops with line supervisors to define the cultural norms and team dynamics necessary for proactive operations. The sessions leveraged constructive conflict and culminated in a strategic plan with a limited number of clear priorities and concrete objectives, each supported by an accountability framework. Trevon then empowered supervisors to run cross-line working groups to refine and hardwire operational tactics. He also worked with the IT team to modernize performance analytics, revised incentives to align with strategic outcomes, and transparently shared progress with stakeholders in real-time. As momentum built, he replaced long meetings with shorter check-ins, delegated certain tasks to high-performing leaders, and deliberately protected time for strategic oversight.

Trevon's leaders quickly began identifying risks before they became crises. The plant shifted from constant reaction to disciplined anticipation, positioning Trevon and his team to proactively plan for future challenges rather than merely enduring them.

Identify Opportunities to Challenge People and Processes

Once you shift from reactive management to proactive leadership, opportunities for Transformational Challenge will become more apparent. While many will be obvious, some of the most valuable will be subtle. Identifying these more nuanced opportunities can be facilitated by a structured and disciplined approach.

In chapter 3, I suggested that the lead in the story of the Master Alchemist represented both people and processes. This book primarily focuses on applying the alchemical leadership formula to people for several reasons.

First, operational preoccupation often leads to organizational neglect, resulting in an overemphasis on refining processes and an underemphasis on developing people. Unless you deliberately prioritize people, organizational neglect is likely. Accordingly, I wanted this book to emphasize relationships and people over tasks and processes.

Second, building exceptionally healthy organizational culture and team dynamics requires a deliberate, top-down focus on supporting and transforming people. I intended the content to position you for success in this endeavor by strongly emphasizing a people-centered approach.

Lastly, it's the people who drive the processes. If you can successfully shift from reactive manager to proactive leader, process refinement can be effectively delegated to other leaders and employees who are better positioned to make meaningful change. This dichotomy conveniently allows you to directly own the transformation of people while indirectly overseeing the transformation of processes as you deem appropriate.

The remainder of this section will divide the process of identifying challenge opportunities into those that apply to people and those that apply to processes.

You can harness the following approaches to identify opportunities to challenge people. As already suggested, they should usually be directly owned and applied.

- Develop a structured language for professional competencies:

  It is difficult to effectively challenge people to improve their professional competencies without a structured language for them. While many exist, I'm particularly fond of the Korn Ferry Leadership Architect model.[51] This approach identifies 38 core competencies and organizes them into the four factors of thought, people, results, and self. For each core competency, the basic skill is conceptually defined, and behavioral descriptors are provided for proficiency levels that are considered less skilled, skilled, highly skilled, or overused. I have found this degree of specificity to be highly valuable in applied leadership development.

- Leverage care in contemplating person-centered opportunities:

  It tends to be relatively easy to identify development opportunities for new and lower-performing employees. It can be far more challenging for seasoned and higher-performing employees.

In the 2007 movie, *Pride*, Philadelphia Department of Recreation swim coach Jim Ellis uses scuba gear to carefully observe his swimmers' technique from the bottom of the pool.[52] This is a useful metaphor for the literally and figuratively "careful" observation required to identify growth opportunities in advanced employees.

In the literal sense, it's important for a leader to be objectively meticulous in the "careful" study of a high-performing employee, looking beneath the surface. In the figurative sense, this requires intentional presence that is "full of care." Essentially, you need to care enough to watch carefully. This allows you to see what you might otherwise miss.

- Ask employees to contemplate person-centered opportunities:

    A highly effective way to challenge employees is to periodically ask them to reflect on their strengths and developmental opportunities and identify steps to improve in both areas. This exercise can be enhanced by the precision that comes from using a structured language for professional competencies.

- Cascade people-centered challenge:

    In a multi-layered organization, senior leaders can create a culture of leadership development by not only applying challenge to their direct reports but also requiring them to do the same for their own teams.

The following techniques can help you identify opportunities to challenge processes. They can often be indirectly overseen and delegated.

- Utilize your strategic plan to evaluate process opportunities:

  Earlier, we addressed the value of creating a strategic plan that includes strategic priorities, objectives, and tactics. Evaluating these discrete components can be an impactful way of identifying opportunities to refine processes. Because tactics involve concrete actions, they can be a particularly fertile area of exploration. You should place emphasis on areas of underperformance, perceived inefficiency, or potential risks.

- Leverage care in contemplating process-centered opportunities:

  As with our discussion of this approach in facilitating person-centered challenge, it's important to carefully examine opportunities for process improvement. This mitigates the risk of operational preoccupation causing strategic autopilot. In other words, careful consideration can prevent you from becoming so busy "doing things" that you don't realize you should either be doing those things differently or doing entirely different things.

- Ask employees to contemplate process-centered opportunities:

  Because it's the people who drive the processes, it is extremely important to ensure that these processes are designed by and for the people. While this may sound obvious, many organizations expend considerable energy designing processes without the input of those who will use them, only to discover they are significantly flawed.

Conversely, there is tremendous practical and cultural value in leveraging employee expertise in process work. You can do this in various ways, including holding process design and refinement meetings where a representative group of participants can collaborate, creating task forces focused on achieving specific goals by implementing novel procedures, and assigning stretch projects or process champion roles to employees who can give heightened attention to critical areas.

- Solicit process improvement feedback:

    The people who use the processes are usually best equipped to provide meaningful feedback. Actively soliciting such feedback for established processes has both practical and cultural value.

The Leadership Journey of Trevon Brooks: Part Two

Following his success in stabilizing operations in his own plant, Trevon was asked to oversee manufacturing operations across multiple plants as a Senior Regional Plant Director. Performance had plateaued, innovation had slowed, operational routines had calcified, and metrics were lagging. Trevon quickly recognized that passivity was a major barrier and that meaningful improvement would require deliberately challenging both people and processes.

Trevon began by sharing his strategic plan with local plant managers, soliciting feedback, refining it collaboratively, and building shared ownership. He then established operational improvement goals for each site and asked managers to engage their teams in identifying the most effective paths to success. In parallel, he partnered with HR team to develop a structured language for core leadership competencies. This enabled Trevon to constructively challenge leaders—coaching development in specific areas, setting expectations, and inviting them to identify their own developmental opportunities.

Teams responded with renewed energy. Managers and frontline employees proposed process improvements, experimented with new production techniques, and openly shared lessons learned across sites. Trevon was encouraged by the shift, but he also recognized that identifying opportunities for challenge was only part of the work. Sustained improvement would require skillfully delivering that challenge, especially when it involved individuals.

Finding the Philosopher's Stone: Practicing Transformational Challenge

Mastering the art of catalyzing individual and organizational change through the active use of Transformational Challenge requires a unique skill set and ongoing practice. Having addressed skill-building, the tactics that follow can be leveraged to enhance your delivery of Transformational Challenge.

- Deliver the challenge in an environment of psychological safety:

    There's a reason the story of the Master Alchemist introduced the Elixir of Life first. Likewise, there's a reason I placed the chapter on Transformational Care before this one. It is typically far easier to accept intense challenge when we also feel intensely cared about. Much of the art of Leadership Alchemy is knowing how to ready someone for intense challenge and knowing when the time is right to apply it.

    In general, you should deliver care first, and with enough consistency to create psychological safety. I mentioned psychological safety in chapter 7 as a technique for altruistic intervention, alluded to it again here in the section on building exceptionally healthy organizational culture and team dynamics, and will address it further in the next chapter. This is because creating psychological safety is critical.

- Deliver the challenge over the appropriate medium and in the appropriate setting:

A leader should exercise great care when choosing between the media of text messages, emails, phone conversations, virtual conversations, and in-person conversations.

With in-person conversations, you should distinguish appropriately between occasions for conversations within vs. outside the work environment. Discussing a major promotion opportunity over lunch at a restaurant, for example, is different from doing so in the hallway between meetings.

Text messaging and emails are usually only appropriate for minor, simple, and encouraging challenges. This is because many of the nuances we have considered can be lost or misconstrued when written. In general, don't let the wrong medium or setting spoil the right message.

- Establish clear goals:

For this task, I recommend using the acronym SMART (Simple, Measurable, Attainable, Relevant, Time-bound), which was popularized by George Dorain in 1981.[50] Deliverables should also be assigned to a specific owner who can be held accountable. Ideally, these goals and deliverables should be taken directly from your strategic plan and objectives.

- Set clear expectations and create accountability:

Clear expectations should be set with all relevant parties, and with sufficient regularity that no one can claim ignorance. You should also use ongoing feedback to hold individuals and teams accountable.

Because complex goals usually require broad participation, one effective organizational tool is the Responsibility Assignment Matrix. It uses the acronym RACI to identify parties who are Responsible, Accountable, Consulted, and Informed.[53] Responsible individuals perform the actual work—the "doers." Accountable individuals are ultimately answerable for successful completion—the "owners." Consulted individuals provide subject matter expertise or stakeholder input—the "advisers." Informed individuals receive updates to maintain awareness and oversight—the "supervisors."

- Require action plans:

  Benjamin Franklin is often credited with saying, "If you fail to plan, you plan to fail." Although there's some controversy about the attribution, the wisdom is indisputable. Even well-defined goals, aligned with strategic objectives, only have value when they are effectively executed. Requiring action plans to utilize SMART goals and apply the RACI matrix to each deliverable clarifies ownership, drives accountability, and facilitates meaningful change.

- Connect the goals to intrinsic motivation:

  Research has clearly demonstrated that intrinsic motivation is a strong driver of success, especially in the face of difficulty. In their book *Switch*, Chip and Dan Heath propose the memorable analogy of an elephant and its rider, illustrating that a leader must both "direct the rider" by setting clear goals and "motivate the elephant" by appealing to intrinsic emotional motivation.[52] Indeed, even if an elephant rider knows where they should go, they won't get far unless the elephant wants to move.

As described in the previous chapter, the altruistic application of Transformational Care is one of the most powerful ways you can stimulate intrinsic motivation.

- Create stretch assignments and designate process champions:

  For several reasons, these approaches can be extremely effective ways of driving change. First, the individuals can be carefully selected for their ideal aptitudes. Second, this introduces a peer-to-peer element that can yield significant change-management benefits. Third, it improves engagement. Just bear in mind that stretch assignments and process champions are most appropriate when the process is already clear and well defined and when the primary goal is to improve awareness, adoption, and implementation.

- Create task forces:

  Creating task forces can be an efficacious way to deliver change for similar reasons. Task forces tend to be most appropriate when the process requires analysis and overhaul, when a cross-functional perspective would be beneficial, when the workload is significant, and when enhanced credibility is required.

- Deliver consistent, timely, and clear feedback about performance:

Performance should be objectively tracked at regular intervals and transparently shared with all relevant parties. Feedback should be given to both teams and individuals, as appropriate. Beyond reporting the actual results, you should add context and provide guidance on recommended actions.

- Provide coaching:

    Research has shown that positive reinforcement (adding a positive stimulus after a desired behavior or outcome) is far more productive than negative reinforcement (removing a noxious stimulus) or punishment (adding a noxious stimulus). You can administer positive reinforcement through private praise, public social recognition, financial and non-financial rewards, and gamification (leaderboards and contests).[1,6,17]

    Shortcomings should be constructively coached. You can accomplish this through constructive feedback, targeted upskilling, peer-to-peer mentoring, 360-degree evaluations, action planning, and performance improvement programs.[6,48]

- Deliver corrective conversations with special care:

    Corrective conversations are focused discussions intended to definitively address specific performance or behavioral deficiencies that fall below minimum standards. Unlike coaching—which is collaborative, future-oriented, encouraging, and developmental—corrective conversations are directive, urgent, higher intensity, and can carry consequences if change does not occur.[6,48]

Effective corrective conversations contain several essential elements. Leaders should clearly identify the behavioral or performance gaps, provide contemporaneous and concrete examples, and clarify expectations. They should also invite employees to share their perspective, identify barriers, and develop solutions. The conversation should culminate in a collaboratively created action or performance improvement plan with defined steps and timelines.[6,48]

I also advise dividing corrective conversations into three phases: preparation, delivery, and follow-through. Preparation requires careful planning of both content and tone and can be strengthened by written talking points. During delivery, leaders should clearly convey the essential elements, appropriately balancing care and challenge and using the talking points as a guide rather than a mechanical script. In the follow-through phase, it's almost always useful to provide the feedback in writing. This allows the employee to reflect on it in a lower intensity setting while establishing a formal record. You should also schedule regular check-ins to reinforce expectations, support progress, and create accountability.

- What you permit, you promote:

    Chronic, unremediated underperformance should be definitively addressed. In some cases, an internal transfer to a role better aligned with the employee's strengths can be appropriate. In other cases, termination may be best for both the individual and the organization. What is rarely beneficial is leaving persistent underperformance unaddressed, as it tends to perpetuate itself. Conversely, managing it with professionalism promotes accountability and excellence.

It's worth mentioning that operational prowess should never be considered sufficient compensation for cultural misbehavior. Bluntly put, being good at one's job shouldn't give one license to treat others badly. Finally, tolerance for one employee's underperformance can have an underappreciated but tremendously detrimental impact on many others. As the saying goes, don't let one rotten apple spoil the whole bushel.

- Deliver the challenge as a servant leader:

  In chapter 7, we explored the power of truly altruistic care, and I suggested that there is a causal relationship between the purity of a leader's altruistic intent and the effectiveness of their care. I believe the same applies to challenge.

  Leaders can knowingly or unknowingly challenge employees for the purpose of reinforcing their sense of superiority and control. This dynamic has been described as dominance-based leadership, ego-defensive leadership, narcissistic leadership, and weaponized feedback.[29]

  Employees can usually sense the difference between selflessly and selfishly motivated challenge. When challenge is used to develop rather than dominate, it tends to increase intrinsic motivation, strengthen trust, enhance learning, and sustainably elevate performance. Conversely, when challenge is used to assert power rather than assist people, it tends to have the opposite effect. To the extent that you unselfishly challenge your employees, they will be more likely to rise to the occasion and reciprocate through higher levels of organizational citizenship.[23,28,29,34,35]

The Leadership Journey of Trevon Brooks: Part Three

As a senior executive, Trevon supervised several high-performing plant managers. One of them was Prieto. While Prieto was a respected and historically reliable leader, he had started to miss key production deadlines and respond defensively to peer feedback. Trevon had worked closely with Prieto for years and had never seen this pattern before. He was concerned not only about his performance, but also about his personal well-being. Confident that he had already established sufficient psychological safety with Prieto, Trevon believed he could successfully address the situation through a thoughtful and direct coaching conversation.

Trevon met privately with Prieto and shared his concerns for both Prieto's performance and wellness. He cited specific examples of missed deadlines and defensive responses and invited Prieto's perspective. Prieto acknowledged the issues and shared that personal challenges at home had been affecting his focus and emotional bandwidth. Trevon listened attentively, expressed genuine concern, offered support resources, and asked what assistance might be helpful. Once it was clear that Prieto felt understood and supported, Trevon clearly reinforced expectations around performance, collaboration, and accountability. He reminded Prieto of his long history of excellence, tapping into Prieto's intrinsic motivation to succeed. Finally, he asked Prieto to develop a structured action plan with measurable deliverables and timelines.

Prieto responded positively, regaining consistency in his performance and re-engaging constructively with his colleagues. Trevon stayed engaged, positively reinforcing progress and gently coaching opportunities. Prieto later thanked Trevon for addressing the situation with compassion while holding him accountable to the standards he knew he was capable of meeting.

Chapter Summary

We began this chapter by recalling the Master Alchemist's description of the Philosopher's Stone: *She claimed that it had to be able to cause a powerful reaction.* We revisited my suggestion that it represented Transformational Challenge and my clarification that Transformational Challenge isn't ordinary challenge. It is challenge, so intensely delivered, that it can trigger a transformation.

We then established that for challenge to be transformational, the opportunity for change must first be internally recognized. We described how this necessitates a shift from reactive management to proactive leadership, and we examined several ways you can accomplish this. These are summarized here:

Shift from Reactive Management to Proactive Leadership

- Build exceptionally healthy organizational culture and team dynamics
- Encourage constructive conflict
- Create a strategic plan, disseminate it, and navigate from it
- Refine and hardwire operational processes and tactics
- Develop sophisticated business analytics and monitor real-time performance
- Protect time for strategic planning and use it to identify defensive issues and offensive opportunities
- Stop having 60- and 30-minute meetings
- Develop leaders, empower them, and delegate appropriately
- Incentivize desired behaviors and outcomes

Next, we examined various strategies to actively identify opportunities to challenge people and processes. These are outlined here:

Actively Identify Opportunities to Challenge People

- Develop a structured language for professional competencies
- Leverage care in contemplating person-centered opportunities
- Ask employees to contemplate person-centered opportunities
- Cascade people-centered challenge

Actively Identify Opportunities to Challenge Processes

- Utilize your strategic plan to evaluate process opportunities
- Leverage care in contemplating process-centered opportunities
- Ask employees to contemplate process-centered opportunities
- Solicit process improvement feedback

Finally, we discussed how Transformational Challenge can be effectively delivered, and we reviewed several practices. These are listed here:

Deliver Challenge Effectively

- Deliver the challenge in an environment of psychological safety
- Deliver the challenge over the appropriate medium and setting
- Establish clear goals
- Set clear expectations and create accountability
- Require action plans
- Connect the goals to intrinsic motivation
- Create stretch assignments and designate process champions
- Create task forces
- Deliver consistent, timely, and clear feedback about performance
- Provide coaching
- Deliver corrective conversations with special care
- What you permit, you promote
- Deliver the challenge as a servant leader

Like Transformational Care, these approaches to cultivating and practicing Transformational Challenge are both practical and powerful. If you apply them consistently, you will come to possess a Philosopher's Stone that drives profound and enduring change in individuals and organizations.

9

FROM LEAD TO GOLD: FACILITATING TRANSMUTATION

Most thought her mad, but a small number of people sought her out.

Nobody ever saw one of her trainees emerge with a horde of gold.

But none of them seemed disappointed.

In fact, they seemed quite delighted.

David Birch

I had two primary jobs over the course of high school. During winter weekends, I worked as a ski instructor and tour director for a local company. During the summers, I was a soccer instructor for various organizations. I learned a tremendous amount about myself from these jobs and am grateful for the experiences.

In the summer between my first and second years, my soccer instructor job was at a private school where children attended a two-week immersion camp. It was a remarkable place, and the camp attracted some outstanding leaders. David Birch was one of them.

David was soft-spoken and unassuming but had a quiet confidence that elicited respect. He was an excellent player and instructor. He was an even more exceptional leader. David sincerely cared about the campers and instructors alike; it was unmistakable. And he ardently challenged us to be better. The combination of his care and challenge created a palpable atmosphere of inspiration. David Birch was another Master Alchemist.

Toward the end of each two-week session, we would divide the children into teams, each with a designated instructor for further training. On the last two days of the session, we held a tournament. At the end of my first two-week session at the camp, I was so proud of the progress my team had made. They were playing phenomenally well, individually and together. I couldn't wait to see them in action.

But in the first game, they fell apart. We lost badly to another team I believed we should have soundly beaten.

As I watched it unfold, I was initially able to maintain my perspective and keep my composure. But after a comedy of errors, I became furious. I called a time-out, ran onto the field, and screamed at the kids, telling them to "get their sh*t together."

This was problematic in several ways. First, getting angry at a bunch of children who were playing a friendly game as a learning exercise was inappropriate. Second, this wasn't the constructive channeling of controlled fervor intended to be a source of inspiration *for* the children; it was a destructive discharge of uncontrolled anger *at* them. Third, some of the kids were so young that the intensity was more than they could handle—one of them cried. Fourth, this was a Christian private school, and swearing was not something we did. Lastly, this was out of character for me, as everyone in the camp knew me to be quite even-keeled.

After the game, David approached me and asked if we could discuss what happened. He said something like:

> *Michael, you are an excellent player and an excellent instructor. I want you to be more than just these things. I want you to be an excellent leader. We both know that what happened out there was not excellent leadership. You might want to think about what went wrong and try to learn from it. I get the sense that it had more to do with things that have happened off the field than with what happened on it.*

What he said about the episode having more to do with things that had happened off the field had immediate resonance. I could tell my anger was grossly out of proportion to the event. It didn't take me long to put the pieces together.

At that point in my life, I was fiercely competitive. I was playing soccer year-round on a travel team. I had elected to play for a neighboring town rather than my hometown because the team was better and the environment was healthier (largely due to vastly different coaching styles). When I entered high school, I learned a painful lesson in political rivalry. An influential member of the high school coaching staff was involved with the rival hometown travel team, and I was benched. Another of my travel teammates who was in the same situation was also benched. I found it infuriating. I was literally sick over it and developed severe gastritis and acid reflux that required medication.

The crux of the issue was that I didn't believe it was fair for someone (in this case, the coach) to use their power to impact someone else unfairly and negatively (in this case, me and my travel teammate). What made it far worse was that no matter how hard I tried to change the situation, I couldn't. As the year progressed, I dealt with it as best I could. But it was mostly through suppression, and I remained angry. Eventually, the school year ended, and I headed off to be an instructor at the soccer camp.

As I pondered David's words, I realized that the scene of my team losing the game had looked enough like my personal predicament that I projected my emotions onto it. I also recognized that I did so unconsciously, and with righteous indignation. In hindsight, it was ridiculous, frightening, and humbling. Ridiculous, because the two situations were extremely different, yet I had connected them. Frightening, because my anger had been so intense and unbridled. And humbling, because I used my power as a coach to hurt others, essentially replicating the behavior I had found to be so unfair. I was relieved to understand what happened. But I also knew that unless I found a way to address my emotions, continuing to suppress them would eventually produce a similar outcome.

This revelation set me on a path of introspection, culminating in the following realizations. Life will inevitably present me with situations that I can't control. In these cases, I can still choose how to respond. My responses will either have a constructive or destructive impact on me and on others. True freedom and power come, not from controlling external circumstances, but from my internal ability to choose how to address them. Choosing constructively will often be easier said than done, but it will be worth it. I needed to start by definitively healing the anger I had been suppressing. Eventually, I did.

Beyond the value of these realizations themselves, the experience also taught me how to actively develop emotional intelligence through self-awareness and self-management. Finally, it demonstrated that ugliness can lead to beauty when approached in the right way.

On Transmutation: Using the Elixir of Life and Philosopher's Stone Together

So far, we have extensively explored the concept of transformation in terms of how to practice Transformational Care and Transformational Challenge independently. But we've only alluded to Transmutation. This chapter will examine Transmutation in detail.

While transformation and Transmutation are similar in that they both involve change, they differ significantly in both nature and degree. Transformation is an external, functional modification in how something looks or operates. Although it involves a shift in appearance, form, or function, the underlying substance is preserved. An example would be transforming a chunk of iron ore into an iron spoon. The process is iterative: we now have a spoon, but the spoon is still made of iron.

Transmutation, by contrast, is an internal, essential reconstitution of what something fundamentally *is*. It entails an alteration in nature, substance, or essence. An example would be transmuting the iron spoon into a gold sword. The process is metamorphic: the spoon is now a sword, and the iron is now gold.

At times, people and processes require only transformation, with the necessary shift being incremental. Sometimes, however, Transmutation is called for, with the desired outcome being a dramatic metamorphosis. The Master Alchemist must have both at their disposal, able to guide gradual evolution through transformation and miraculous change through Transmutation.

Either Transformational Care or Challenge alone, when applied with sufficient intensity, can facilitate transformation. Transmutation, however, usually requires the intentional combination of both.

Because care and challenge have different natures, the aspiring alchemist should be mindful of certain pitfalls that can cause the application of one to blunt the other. This chapter will first explore these pitfalls and then explain how to utilize Transformational Care and Transformational Challenge synergistically.

CARE SHOULD NOT DIMINISH CHALLENGE

This is a common pitfall that stems from a confusion between what is nice and what is caring. Being "nice" often serves as a social strategy to maintain harmony, avoid conflict, or gain approval. In this context, necessary challenges are frequently avoided. In contrast, being "caring" is a genuine commitment to another person's welfare, even if it requires difficult honesty. Challenging someone is often the caring choice, while avoiding challenge can be uncaring.

Leaders can make the mistake of withholding challenge due to this misunderstanding in three primary ways: avoiding it altogether, watering it down, or sugarcoating it. Because avoiding these missteps can be difficult, the following are some strategies you can use to ensure that care doesn't diminish challenge.

- Accept that being "nice" can be counterproductive to servant-leadership:

Your job as a servant leader is not to be "nice"—it is to support and empower others. Withholding challenging feedback can deprive employees of the opportunity to grow. It can also be a form of short-term self-protection that causes long-term harm to others.

- Get comfortable with making people uncomfortable:

No matter how gracefully you deliver feedback, challenge can be inherently uncomfortable for others. Because challenge is a professional responsibility, you need to become comfortable with making people uncomfortable.

- Reframe challenge as kindness, not cruelty:

Appropriately challenging employees gives them the opportunity to grow. This is kind. Avoiding challenge because it's personally uncomfortable deprives the employee of the opportunity to grow. This is selfish and cruel. If you are prone to this pitfall, let these facts sink in.

- Provide ongoing microfeedback:

This reduces the intensity of the required feedback as it allows the employee to make small adjustments rather than the sweeping changes that longer feedback intervals can entail. It can also prevent you from accumulating frustration as a leader.

- Be contemporaneous, specific, and objective:

Providing feedback in real-time, linking it to specific events or outcomes, and using objective standards of measurement makes it clearer, more understand-able, and easier to accept.

- Emphasize shared goals and standards:

  This creates a sense of collaboration as opposed to confrontation.

- Be soft on the person and hard on the issues:

  This concept is most often credited to the founders of the Harvard Negotiation Project, who popularized it in their 1981 book, *Getting to Yes: Negotiating Agreement Without Giving In.*[53] Differentiating between the person and the problem allows you to maintain warm, soft, subjectivity for the individual while addressing the issues with cold, hard, objectivity. Doing this fluently makes it easier to deliver challenging feedback without holding back or sugarcoating. David Birch did this effectively when he coupled care for me as a person with a confrontation of my problematic behavior, challenging me to learn from the experience.

The Leadership Journey of Dr. Grace Chen: Part One

Dr. Grace Chen was a Senior Program Manager at a biotechnology firm, leading a cross-functional team on a high-stakes therapeutic development project. The team had never faced a challenge of this magnitude before, and it was clear to Grace that they doubted their ability to succeed. This realization forced her to confront a familiar pattern in her own leadership. While she was deeply appreciated for her warmth and support, she recognized that her natural inclination toward caretaking had made her hesitant to push team members out of their comfort zones. Over time, this reluctance unintentionally allowed complacency to set in. In the current context, she knew that success would require her to get comfortable with making people uncomfortable.

Grace internally reframed challenge as an expression of care and an obligation of servant leadership. She began providing specific microfeedback in real time, clearly identifying gaps between expectations and performance. She framed her feedback as a commitment to both individual and collective success, emphasizing shared organizational goals and standards. She maintained psychological safety by staying soft on the person—listening carefully, validating effort, and preserving dignity—while being firm and consistent about timelines, quality, and accountability.

Soon, team members became excited to stretch and grow. Quality improved, timelines stabilized, and the team developed confidence in their ability to navigate the daunting challenge. Grace learned that when she intentionally balanced care with challenge, she could elevate performance without eroding relationships.

Challenge Should Not Diminish Care

This is also a common pitfall, rooted in the conflation of the problem with the person. It is indisputable that performance can be problematic and behavior can be distasteful. It is equally true, however, that we can care for the person even if we don't care for the performance or behavior. Putting the two together, it's essential to differentiate between the person and their actions so care is not withdrawn during times of challenge.

Because avoiding this pitfall if often easier said than done, here are some strategies you can employ to ensure that challenge does not diminish care.

- Be hard on the issues and soft on the person:

    Again, you can be simultaneously cold, hard, and objective on the issues but warm, soft, and subjective to the person. Doing this with mastery makes it easier to deliver challenging feedback without withdrawing care. It also makes it easier for employees to hear it.

- Differentiate between the problem and the person:

    Internally, this involves regulating your thoughts and feelings such that they are appropriate for the person and the problem. For example, discontent, distaste, and frustration should be directed to the behavior or the outcome, not the person. Externally, this looks like using language that labels the behavior or performance as problematic rather than the person.

- Express care explicitly:

    It can be helpful to state that you're providing the feedback *because* you care. This can be accomplished by saying something like, "I'm going to give you some constructive feedback because I care about your development." You can even add something like, "And I'm deliberately going to be hard on the issues while being soft on you."

- Be verbally and non-verbally warm:

    Using warm verbal and non-verbal language reinforces the explicit expression of care. It's important to note, however, that this warmth shouldn't be applied in a way that softens the challenge. As we will discuss shortly, it should instead allow you to amplify the challenge.

- Appropriately separate intent from impact:

    When appropriate, it can be helpful to acknowledge the positive intent of the employee, before addressing the negative impact of the performance or behavior. This allows you to confront the undesirable outcome while reinforcing the constructive motive.

- Collaborate on next steps:

    Working together to create a path forward fosters collaboration rather than confrontation, shifts the emphasis to future improvement, and empowers the employee to drive the improvement.

The Leadership Journey of Dr. Grace Chen: Part Two

Many months later, Dr. Chen was leading a different therapeutic program under intense regulatory scrutiny. One of her most experienced scientists, Philip, had begun pushing back on protocols, making avoidable errors, and missing documentation deadlines. Grace grew increasingly frustrated. In her urgency to address the issue, she became curt and transactional in her interactions. Without realizing it, she began treating Philip's performance and behavioral issues as a reflection of his character and commitment, withdrawing the warmth and care she typically demonstrated. Philip, in turn, become disengaged and defensive.

After a particularly strained interaction, Grace recognized that she had mistakenly conflated the problem with the person. She scheduled a private conversation and sincerely apologized. She explicitly stated that she cared about Philip, respected his character, and valued his contributions. She then clearly differentiated the specific performance and behavioral gaps from Philip as a person and acknowledged his positive intent. During the conversation, she softened her tone, maintained warm body language, and collaborated with Philip to identify next steps.

Philip responded with visible relief and renewed engagement. He acknowledged the issues, explained the pressures he had been navigating, and committed to the agreed-upon plan. Protocol compliance improved, work quality was sustained, and documentation deadlines were met. Grace reflected on her own leadership journey. She realized that while her natural inclination toward caring had once limited her willingness to issue challenge, frustration had now caused her to withdraw care when confronting underperformance. She recommitted to the discipline of being simultaneously soft on the person and hard on the issues.

Using the Elixir of Life and the Philosopher's Stone Synergistically

Leading change is inherently difficult, particularly when leaders are expected to deliver results while simultaneously sustaining engagement and alignment. Much of conventional leadership advice implicitly frames this as a choice: prioritize performance or prioritize people. The most effective leaders, however, recognize this as a false dichotomy. They understand that the real challenge—and opportunity—is to achieve both, simultaneously and consistently.

It is therefore not coincidental that the concept of being hard on the issues and soft on the person emerged as a technique for avoiding both pitfalls described earlier in this chapter. This approach is more than just a safeguard against transmutational failure—it is the critical determinant of transmutational success because it creates synergy.

Delivering Transformational Care and Challenge consistently over time generates this synergy through a cycle of mutual reinforcement. When a leader is consistently soft on the person, they can be even harder on the issues. Leaders tend to feel more comfortable delivering rigorous feedback when they know they have consistently demonstrated care. Employees, in turn, are generally more receptive when they know that the challenge comes from a place of care.

Similarly, when a leader is consistently hard on the issues, they can be even softer on the person. Leaders usually feel more confident expressing care when they know they have also held people accountable. And employees are also more likely to find that care credible when they know they have also been challenged.

This reciprocal dynamic, in which each element strengthens the other, produces a rhythm of leadership that is both high-support and high-expectation. Rather than forcing a trade-off between results and relationships, each becomes an amplifier of the other.

In practice, I have found I can push my teams more effectively when they know I genuinely care about them. Conversely, I can express care more generously and with greater impact when they know I also challenge them. By harnessing this synergy, I have been able to intensively drive performance while simultaneously deepening engagement.

In contrast, the isolated longitudinal application of care or challenge alone, without the complement of the other, is almost always detrimental. Consistent softness toward the person without hardness on the issues is likely to discredit the care and foster underperformance. And consistent hardness on the issues without softness for the person is unlikely to produce sustained performance improvement because it tends to erode engagement.

A useful analysis of the hard on the issues and soft on the person concept involves creating a matrix that includes the four potential leadership approaches of: 1) Hard on the issues and hard on the person; 2) Hard on the person and soft on the issues; 3) Soft on the issues and soft on the person, and 4) Hard on the issues and soft on the person. I call this the "Hard on the Issues and Soft on the Person Matrix," and I like to whimsically associate it with "Leadership Merit Badges."

The Hard on the Issue and Soft on the Person Matrix

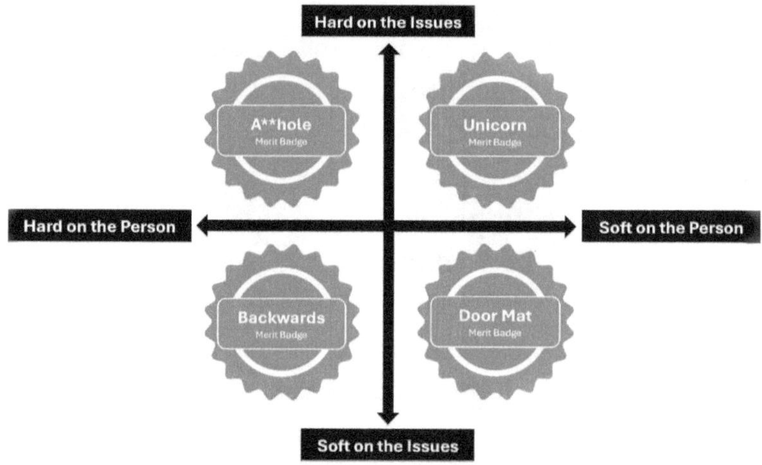

Being hard on the issues and hard on the person can earn a leader the A**hole Merit Badge. Being soft on the issues and hard on the person can earn a leader the Backwards Merit Badge. Being soft on the issues and soft on the person can earn a leader the Doormat Merit Badge. The point here is obvious—don't be an a**hole, don't be backwards, and don't be a doormat. What you should strive for is the Unicorn Merit Badge. Mixing the metaphors, Master Alchemists are unicorns.

At this point, we have established that successful Transmutation usually can't occur without both Transformational Care and Challenge. So far, the discussion has appropriately focused on delivering them consistently over time, as transmutational change is most commonly the product of their sustained application. In this long view, however, while each should be a constant component of a leader's overall approach, certain moments call for emphasizing one over the other. Said another way, there are times when an employee needs more care than challenge, and there are times when an employee needs more challenge than care.

An emphasis on care tends to be called for when onboarding or mentoring, during stress, after setbacks or failures, and when recognizing or celebrating. An emphasis on challenge tends to be more appropriate when addressing development and growth, when stakes are high, and when an employee is performing below potential.

Certain moments also require titration of the intensity of the care or challenge. Intensification may be required when success is imperative, in times of crisis, if inertia needs to be overcome, or when you sense a teachable moment. Softening may be required after such times of intensification to allow individuals and teams to assimilate the lessons learned.

You should also give thoughtful attention to individually customizing transmutational interventions to maximize their effectiveness. Individuals differ widely in their desire and capacity to change. Employees with the greatest desire and capacity to change can handle more intense applications of Transformational Care and Challenge.

People also vary greatly in which approaches will be most effective, based on their unique motivations, learning styles, experiences, backgrounds, and developmental receptivity. All of these factors influence how they will respond to care and challenge. Psychologist and leadership scholar Bernard Bass described this kind of customization as "Individualized Consideration" and recognized it as one of four critical elements in his theory of *Transformational Leadership*.[54]

An essential aspect of individualized consideration in today's multigenerational business environment is recognizing and responding to generational differences, including life and work goals, values and priorities, communication styles, feedback and recognition preferences, learning approaches, developmental expectations, technology use, and attitudes about authority and collaboration. In their 2025 book, *Genfluence: How to Lead a Multigenerational Workforce*, authors Meese and Collard compellingly argue that "when leaders embrace generational diversity not as a problem to be managed but an asset to be leveraged, they unlock untapped reservoirs of talent, creativity, and commitment."[55]

These principles of longitudinal consistency, variable emphasis, variable intensity, and individual customization can be summarized as follows:

- Deliver Transformational Care and Challenge with longitudinal consistency.

- Emphasize Transformational Care or Challenge in the moment, depending on the person and the situation.

- Titrate the intensity of the Transformational Care and Challenge in the moment, depending on the person and the situation.

- Customize Transformational Care and Challenge based on individual variation.

The Leadership Journey of Dr. Grace Chen: Part Three

Several years later, Grace was appointed to lead a large portfolio of therapeutic programs during a period of organizational restructuring and aggressive growth expectations. The scope and implications were unprecedented. Some teams were overwhelmed by the pace of change, others were underperforming, and a few high-potential individuals were capable of more than they were delivering. Grace recognized that success would require more than consistent care or challenge alone—it would require intentionally weaving both together over time, with precision and adaptability.

Drawing on hard-earned experience, Grace delivered care and challenge with longitudinal consistency, while varying emphasis, intensity, and approach based on situational context and individual needs. During onboarding, setbacks, and periods of acute stress, she emphasized care—coaching closely, acknowledging effort, and creating space for learning. When stakes were high or performance lagged, she leaned into challenge—clearly defining expectations, setting ambitious goals, and holding teams and individuals accountable. She amplified intensity during critical regulatory milestones and softened afterward to allow assimilation. With some team members she pushed aggressively, knowing they could handle it. With others she led more gently, tailoring her approach based on motivation, experience, and developmental readiness.

In time, a powerful cycle of reinforcement emerged. Because Grace was consistently soft on the person, teams became increasingly receptive to intense challenge. And because she was reliably hard on the issues, her expressions of care felt credible and earned. Engagement increased, performance improved, and the organization successfully navigated the transformation with improved resilience. Grace's leadership now reflected true mastery: the ability to integrate care and challenge so seamlessly that each amplified the other, producing dynamic and lasting change.

Once you've learned to use the Elixir of Life and the Philosopher's Stone synergistically, many things that seemed previously out of reach will become quite attainable. You'll be able to facilitate gradual transformation when incremental growth is appropriate, while sparking Transmutation when miraculous change is required.

In doing so, you will be in command of the "two simple things" that Nurse Bonnie believed "good leadership" always came down to. That day on the ski lift, she colorfully characterized them as "actually giving a sh*t" and "actually making sh*t better." With her trademark bluntness, Nurse Bonnie was describing the essential leadership truths of Transformational Care and Transformational Challenge.

While I didn't have time to ask her, I'm confident that it was the masterful combination of both care and challenge that drove the outstanding leadership she admitted several hospitals had displayed. As *you* adopt this transmutational approach, processes will certainly respond. But more importantly, people will blossom in extraordinary ways. And as in the story of the Master Alchemist, the treasure they carry away from their experience with you will be worth far more than gold.

Chapter Summary

We began this chapter by differentiating between transformation and Transmutation, with transformation resulting in external, functional, and iterative change and Transmutation resulting in internal, essential, and dramatic change. We clarified that while transformation can be caused by either Transformational Care or Transformational Challenge alone, Transmutation usually requires both.

We then recognized the need to ensure that care doesn't diminish challenge and discussed several practices. These are summarized here:

Ensure That Care Does Not Diminish Challenge

- Accept that being "nice" can be counterproductive to servant-leadership
- Get comfortable with making people uncomfortable
- Reframe challenge as kindness, not cruelty
- Provide ongoing microfeedback
- Be contemporaneous, specific, and objective
- Emphasize shared goals and standards
- Be soft on the person and hard on the issues

Next, we acknowledged the need to ensure that challenge doesn't diminish care and reviewed several approaches. These are listed here:

Ensure That Challenge Does Not Diminish Care

- Be hard on the issues and soft on the person
- Differentiate between the problem and the person
- Express care explicitly
- Be verbally and non-verbally warm
- Appropriately separate intent from impact
- Collaborate on next steps

Finally, we described the synergistic use of Transformational Care and Transformational Challenge and described several tactics. These are outlined here:

Deliver Care and Challenge Synergistically

- Utilize longitudinal consistency
- Employ variable emphasis
- Use variable intensity
- Provide individual customization

As you gain mastery in integrating Transformational Care and Transformational Challenge, you will develop the capacity to intentionally shape both performance and possibility. You will hold the keys to unlocking latent potential within people and processes—ultimately bringing the allegorical story of the Master Alchemist to life.

The Personal Characteristics of Master Alchemists

This book has deliberately said much about what Master Alchemists do, but little about who they are. This is primarily because Leadership Alchemy is not about the alchemists themselves; it's about serving others. Before moving to Part Three, though, I will briefly comment on the personal characteristics of Master Alchemists, using Uncle Kurt and David Birch as two distinct examples.

In the case of Uncle Kurt, the transmutation was exceptionally profound. It occurred after many years of Kurt providing alternating doses of Transformational Care and Challenge. Each dose was small, and it took time for the accumulation to trigger a transmutation. When it occurred, the trigger was indirect: it was not Kurt who provided the substrate for the lesson (he wasn't the source of joy and connectedness). Finally, Kurt was an informal leader in my life without a clear responsibility to teach me.

With David Birch, while the transmutation that occurred was highly valuable, it was far less profound. It occurred in a single interaction. The dose was large enough to instantly trigger a transmutation. When it occurred, the trigger was direct: it was David who provided the substrate for the lesson. Finally, David was a formal leader in my life with a clear responsibility to teach me.

These disparate examples illustrate that Leadership Alchemy can produce minor or major transmutations, unfold slowly or quickly, act as a direct or indirect source of growth, and have formal or informal sources.

Regarding personal characteristics, Kurt and David had vastly different physical appearances, backgrounds, professions, personalities, beliefs, values, cognitive approaches, and communication styles. This demonstrates that Master Alchemists can vary greatly on the inside and the outside.

The most significant personal characteristic that they shared was a high degree of self-mastery, marked by wholeness and selflessness. These are requirements of all Master Alchemists. Self-mastery needs to be cultivated. Fortunately, when approached with humility, leadership mastery and self-mastery are complementary pursuits.

It is my hope that while this book focuses on leadership mastery, it will also serve you well in your pursuit of self-mastery.

PART THREE
Moving from Theory to Practice

In Part One, we explored the timeless story of the Master Alchemist, contemplated its allegorical meaning, introduced the alchemical leadership formula, and examined the history of alchemy. In Part Two, we focused on the key elements of the story: the Master Alchemist (You), the Elixir of Life (Transformational Care), and the Philosopher's Stone (Transformational Challenge). We also discussed the proper approach to achieving Transmutation.

Part Three is designed to promote self-reflection and self-development. Each of the four chapters will sequentially focus on the critical elements of being a Master Alchemist, applying the Elixir of Life, using the Philosopher's Stone, and effecting Transmutation. You will assess your level of mastery across these elements, along with your use of the associated techniques and practices. You will then identify specific steps you can take to develop greater proficiency. I've left you space to do so. As in chapter 2, if you would prefer not to write, you may certainly think through your responses instead. You can also choose to skip this section.

I suggest approaching this exercise with the understanding that a mastery of leadership alchemy begins with a mastery of self. Such self-mastery necessitates that both Transformational Care and Challenge are applied inwardly, with sufficient intensity and consistency to facilitate Transmutation. Reflecting on the questions with a balance care and challenge, without allowing one to diminish the other, will help you get the most out of the experience.

10

SELF-REFLECTION ON BEING A MASTER ALCHEMIST

For the questions that follow, rate yourself on a scale of 1 to 10, with 1 being beginner level alchemy and 10 being master level alchemy. For questions where you have room for improvement, think about what specific steps you can take to become more adept. This self-reflection exercise corresponds to the material in chapter 6.

- Am I mentally and emotionally comfortable holding authority?

1	2	3	4	5	6	7	8	9	10

- Do I hold myself accountable for transforming and transmuting processes?

1	2	3	4	5	6	7	8	9	10

- Do I hold myself accountable for transforming and transmuting people?

1	2	3	4	5	6	7	8	9	10

- Do I consistently and effectively apply the alchemical leadership formula?

1	2	3	4	5	6	7	8	9	10

The Alchemical Leadership Formula

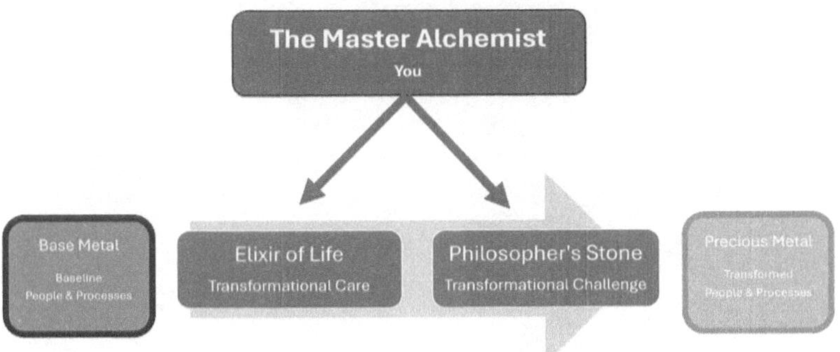

11

SELF-REFLECTION ON USING THE ELIXIR OF LIFE

For the questions that follow, rate yourself on a scale of 1 to 10, with 1 being beginner level alchemy and 10 being master level alchemy. For questions where you have room for improvement, think about what specific steps you can take to become more adept. This self-reflection exercise corresponds to the material in chapter 7.

- Do I authentically care about my employees?

| 1 | 2 | 3 | 4 | 5 | 6 | 7 | 8 | 9 | 10 |

- Do I effectively express the care I have for them?

| 1 | 2 | 3 | 4 | 5 | 6 | 7 | 8 | 9 | 10 |

- Do my employees know that I authentically care for them?

| 1 | 2 | 3 | 4 | 5 | 6 | 7 | 8 | 9 | 10 |

- Are people transforming because of my care for them?

| 1 | 2 | 3 | 4 | 5 | 6 | 7 | 8 | 9 | 10 |

How effectively am I utilizing the techniques that follow?

Personal Wellness

- Practice self-care

| 1 | 2 | 3 | 4 | 5 | 6 | 7 | 8 | 9 | 10 |

- Build personal emotional competence

| 1 | 2 | 3 | 4 | 5 | 6 | 7 | 8 | 9 | 10 |

EMPATHY

- Develop fluency in my own emotions

| 1 | 2 | 3 | 4 | 5 | 6 | 7 | 8 | 9 | 10 |

- Practice active listening

| 1 | 2 | 3 | 4 | 5 | 6 | 7 | 8 | 9 | 10 |

- Employ perspective-taking

| 1 | 2 | 3 | 4 | 5 | 6 | 7 | 8 | 9 | 10 |

- Observe and interpret emotional cues

| 1 | 2 | 3 | 4 | 5 | 6 | 7 | 8 | 9 | 10 |

- Avoid judgment

| 1 | 2 | 3 | 4 | 5 | 6 | 7 | 8 | 9 | 10 |

- Solicit feedback

| 1 | 2 | 3 | 4 | 5 | 6 | 7 | 8 | 9 | 10 |

- Avoid emotional contagion

1	2	3	4	5	6	7	8	9	10

- Develop comfort with my own emotions

1	2	3	4	5	6	7	8	9	10

- Have emotional presence0

1	2	3	4	5	6	7	8	9	10

- Utilize validation

1	2	3	4	5	6	7	8	9	10

- Avoid empathic distress

1	2	3	4	5	6	7	8	9	10

Compassion

- Adopt a servant leader mindset and heart-set

1	2	3	4	5	6	7	8	9	10

- Pay it forward

1	2	3	4	5	6	7	8	9	10

- Adopt a compassionate pedagogy

1	2	3	4	5	6	7	8	9	10

- Avoid compassion fatigue

1	2	3	4	5	6	7	8	9	10

- Practice radical acceptance

1	2	3	4	5	6	7	8	9	10

- Distinguish between empowering support and dis-empowering rescue

1	2	3	4	5	6	7	8	9	10

ALTRUISTIC INTERVENTION

- Create a culture of care and psychological safety

1	2	3	4	5	6	7	8	9	10

- Strive for cumulative continuity

1	2	3	4	5	6	7	8	9	10

- Look for ways to both provide benefit and reduce hassle

1	2	3	4	5	6	7	8	9	10

- Practice principled altruism

1	2	3	4	5	6	7	8	9	10

- Maintain fairness and justice

1	2	3	4	5	6	7	8	9	10

Transparent Non-verbal Communication of Care

- Body language

1	2	3	4	5	6	7	8	9	10

- Facial expression

1	2	3	4	5	6	7	8	9	10

- Eye behavior

1	2	3	4	5	6	7	8	9	10

- Paralanguage

1	2	3	4	5	6	7	8	9	10

- Appearance and artifacts

1	2	3	4	5	6	7	8	9	10

- Use of space

1	2	3	4	5	6	7	8	9	10

- Appropriate touch

1	2	3	4	5	6	7	8	9	10

- Use of time

1	2	3	4	5	6	7	8	9	10

TRANSPARENT VERBAL COMMUNICATION OF CARE

- Tell employees that I care about their professional well-being

1	2	3	4	5	6	7	8	9	10

- Provide recognition

1	2	3	4	5	6	7	8	9	10

- Celebrate success

1	2	3	4	5	6	7	8	9	10

- Provide support and encouragement during times of struggle and disappointment

| 1 | 2 | 3 | 4 | 5 | 6 | 7 | 8 | 9 | 10 |

- Tell employees that I care about their personal well-being

| 1 | 2 | 3 | 4 | 5 | 6 | 7 | 8 | 9 | 10 |

HUMBLE RECEPTIVITY

- Make it more important to get it right than to be right

| 1 | 2 | 3 | 4 | 5 | 6 | 7 | 8 | 9 | 10 |

- Have an open-door policy

| 1 | 2 | 3 | 4 | 5 | 6 | 7 | 8 | 9 | 10 |

- Seek feedback

| 1 | 2 | 3 | 4 | 5 | 6 | 7 | 8 | 9 | 10 |

- Accept and value feedback

| 1 | 2 | 3 | 4 | 5 | 6 | 7 | 8 | 9 | 10 |

- Be vulnerable

| 1 | 2 | 3 | 4 | 5 | 6 | 7 | 8 | 9 | 10 |

Drawing on the chapter material and my previous reflections, the top three aspects of Transformational Care I will focus on improving are:

1. ____

2. ____

3. ____

12
SELF-REFLECTION ON USING THE PHILOSOPHER'S STONE

For the questions that follow, rate yourself on a scale of 1 to 10, with 1 being beginner level alchemy and 10 being master level alchemy. For questions where you have room for improvement, think about what specific steps you can take to become more adept. This self-reflection exercise corresponds to the material in chapter 8.

- Am I more of a proactive leader than a reactive manager?

1	2	3	4	5	6	7	8	9	10

- Do I challenge my employees?

1	2	3	4	5	6	7	8	9	10

- Are people transforming because of my challenges?

1	2	3	4	5	6	7	8	9	10

- Do I challenge processes?

1	2	3	4	5	6	7	8	9	10

- Are processes transforming because of my challenges?

1	2	3	4	5	6	7	8	9	10

How effectively am I utilizing the tactics that follow?

Shift from Reactive Management to Proactive Leadership

- Build exceptionally healthy organizational culture and team dynamics

1	2	3	4	5	6	7	8	9	10

- Encourage constructive conflict

1	2	3	4	5	6	7	8	9	10

- Create a strategic plan, disseminate it, and navigate from it

1	2	3	4	5	6	7	8	9	10

- Refine and hardwire operational processes and tactics

1	2	3	4	5	6	7	8	9	10

- Develop sophisticated business analytics and monitor real-time performance

1	2	3	4	5	6	7	8	9	10

- Protect time for strategic planning and use it to identify defensive issues and offensive opportunities

1	2	3	4	5	6	7	8	9	10

- Stop having 60- and 30-minute meetings

| 1 | 2 | 3 | 4 | 5 | 6 | 7 | 8 | 9 | 10 |

- Develop leaders, empower them, and delegate appropriately

| 1 | 2 | 3 | 4 | 5 | 6 | 7 | 8 | 9 | 10 |

- Incentivize desired behaviors and outcomes

| 1 | 2 | 3 | 4 | 5 | 6 | 7 | 8 | 9 | 10 |

ACTIVELY IDENTIFY OPPORTUNITIES TO CHALLENGE PEOPLE

- Develop a structured language for professional competencies

| 1 | 2 | 3 | 4 | 5 | 6 | 7 | 8 | 9 | 10 |

- Leverage care in contemplating person-centered opportunities

| 1 | 2 | 3 | 4 | 5 | 6 | 7 | 8 | 9 | 10 |

- Ask employees to contemplate person-centered opportunities

| 1 | 2 | 3 | 4 | 5 | 6 | 7 | 8 | 9 | 10 |

- Cascade people-centered challenge

1	2	3	4	5	6	7	8	9	10

ACTIVELY IDENTIFY OPPORTUNITIES TO CHALLENGE PROCESSES

- Utilize my strategic plan to evaluate process opportunities

1	2	3	4	5	6	7	8	9	10

- Leverage care in contemplating process-centered opportunities

1	2	3	4	5	6	7	8	9	10

- Ask employees to contemplate process-centered opportunities

1	2	3	4	5	6	7	8	9	10

- Solicit process improvement feedback

1	2	3	4	5	6	7	8	9	10

DELIVER CHALLENGE EFFECTIVELY

- Deliver the challenge in an environment of psychological safety

1	2	3	4	5	6	7	8	9	10

- Deliver the challenge over the appropriate medium and setting

1	2	3	4	5	6	7	8	9	10

- Establish clear goals

1	2	3	4	5	6	7	8	9	10

- Set clear expectations and create accountability

1	2	3	4	5	6	7	8	9	10

- Require action plans

1	2	3	4	5	6	7	8	9	10

- Connect the goals to intrinsic motivation

1	2	3	4	5	6	7	8	9	10

- Create stretch assignments and designate process champions

1	2	3	4	5	6	7	8	9	10

- Create task forces

1	2	3	4	5	6	7	8	9	10

- Deliver consistent, timely, and clear feedback about performance

| 1 | 2 | 3 | 4 | 5 | 6 | 7 | 8 | 9 | 10 |

- Provide coaching

| 1 | 2 | 3 | 4 | 5 | 6 | 7 | 8 | 9 | 10 |

- Deliver corrective conversations with special care

| 1 | 2 | 3 | 4 | 5 | 6 | 7 | 8 | 9 | 10 |

- What you permit, you promote

| 1 | 2 | 3 | 4 | 5 | 6 | 7 | 8 | 9 | 10 |

- Deliver the challenge as a servant leader

| 1 | 2 | 3 | 4 | 5 | 6 | 7 | 8 | 9 | 10 |

Drawing on the chapter material and my previous reflections, the top three aspects of Transformational Challenge I will focus on improving are:

1. ____

2. ____

3. ____

13

SELF-REFLECTION ON FACILITATING TRANSMUTATION

For the questions that follow, rate yourself on a scale of 1 to 10, with 1 being beginner level alchemy and 10 being master level alchemy. For questions where you have room for improvement, think about what specific steps you can take to become more adept. This self-reflection exercise corresponds to the material in chapter 9.

- Do I avoid, water down, or sugarcoat constructive feedback?

1	2	3	4	5	6	7	8	9	10

- Do I withdraw care when performance is problematic, or behavior is distasteful?

1	2	3	4	5	6	7	8	9	10

- Are there times when I earn the Asshole Merit Badge?

1	2	3	4	5	6	7	8	9	10

- Are there times when I earn the Backwards Merit Badge?

1	2	3	4	5	6	7	8	9	10

- Are there times when I earn the Doormat Merit Badge?

1	2	3	4	5	6	7	8	9	10

How effectively am I utilizing the approaches that follow?

Ensure That Care Does Not Diminish Challenge

- Accept that being "nice" can be counterproductive to servant-leadership

1	2	3	4	5	6	7	8	9	10

- Get comfortable with making people uncomfortable

1	2	3	4	5	6	7	8	9	10

- Reframe challenge as kindness, not cruelty

1	2	3	4	5	6	7	8	9	10

- Provide ongoing microfeedback

1	2	3	4	5	6	7	8	9	10

- Be contemporaneous, specific, and objective

1	2	3	4	5	6	7	8	9	10

- Emphasize shared goals and standards

1	2	3	4	5	6	7	8	9	10

- Be soft on the person and hard on the issues

1	2	3	4	5	6	7	8	9	10

ENSURE THAT CHALLENGE DOES NOT DIMINISH CARE

- Be hard on the issues and soft on the person

1	2	3	4	5	6	7	8	9	10

- Differentiate between the problem and the person

1	2	3	4	5	6	7	8	9	10

- Express care explicitly

1	2	3	4	5	6	7	8	9	10

- Be verbally and non-verbally warm

1	2	3	4	5	6	7	8	9	10

- Appropriately separate intent from impact

1	2	3	4	5	6	7	8	9	10

- Collaborate on next steps

1	2	3	4	5	6	7	8	9	10

Deliver Care and Challenge Synergistically

- Utilize longitudinal consistency

| 1 | 2 | 3 | 4 | 5 | 6 | 7 | 8 | 9 | 10 |

- Employ variable emphasis

| 1 | 2 | 3 | 4 | 5 | 6 | 7 | 8 | 9 | 10 |

- Use variable intensity

| 1 | 2 | 3 | 4 | 5 | 6 | 7 | 8 | 9 | 10 |

- Provide individual customization

| 1 | 2 | 3 | 4 | 5 | 6 | 7 | 8 | 9 | 10 |

Drawing on the chapter material and my previous reflections, the top three aspects of Transmutation I will focus on improving are:

1. ____

2. ____

3. ____

14
PARTING INSTRUCTIONS

Now that you've identified your key areas for growth in being a Master Alchemist, providing Transformational Care, delivering Transformational Challenge, and effecting Transmutation, it's time to turn insight into action. I suggest creating a structured action plan for each focus area, supported by SMART goals as described in chapter 8. You might also consider sharing your learnings with a trusted colleague and inviting their perspective.

Finally, I recommend that you approach this endeavor with a balance of grit and grace, pairing disciplined persistence with the understanding that perfection is a process. Becoming a Master Alchemist doesn't happen overnight. But with consistent practice, you will gain greater mastery each day.

CONCLUSION

The personal vignettes featured in this book represent my recollection of actual events that were both formative in my life and illustrated the concepts I wanted to feature. While the names of the associated individuals were altered to protect their privacy, I didn't materially change what they did or said.

After I selected the stories, I realized that only one of them (David Birch) occurred in a purely professional setting. Because this is a book about professional leadership, I briefly considered using alternative examples. I quickly dismissed the idea for two reasons. First, I wanted this work to be authentic, spontaneous, and heartfelt. Revising the stories felt inconsistent with these goals. Second, the inadvertent inclusion of anecdotes from the personal setting in a book dedicated to professional leadership underscores the inextricable connection between the personal and the professional. We are who we are, and this manifests in our personal and professional lives. As we strive to develop as people and as leaders, the lessons we learn in the personal and professional spheres ideally lead to meaningful growth in both. This has certainly been the case for me, and I hope that it has been and continues to be for you.

I also noticed that the stories emphasized my early life. I'm fortunate that I've also had many meaningful interactions with influential figures later in life. But for the same reasons, I elected to leave the selection unchanged. It's also easier to safeguard anonymity when the events are more distant. Because the previous chapters haven't covered it, though, I will now summarize the rest of my professional journey.

After finishing medical school in 2001, I completed Internal Medicine and Emergency Medicine residencies at Yale New Haven Hospital and went on to practice as a board-certified Emergency Physician and Hospitalist across multiple facilities in Connecticut, New York, North Carolina, and Tennessee. Eventually, I became involved in healthcare administration and obtained an MBA from Louisiana State University. I have served in various executive leadership positions for over 15 years.

Including residency, I had the great privilege of caring for patients for about 22 years before retiring from clinical practice in 2023 to focus exclusively on leadership. Since my clinical retirement, I have missed being at the bedside with other members of the healthcare team and vividly seeing the difference we made for patients and their loved ones. It has also become increasingly clear to me that patients, clinicians, and healthcare workers need more leadership than ever. It has been an immense joy for me to collaborate with so many incredibly dedicated and talented leaders in providing this support.

One of my favorite quotes on life and leadership is from Ralph Waldo Emerson: "To know even one life has breathed easier because you have lived—that is to have succeeded." One of my own reads: "Some see the glass as half full. Some see the glass as half empty. Others pick it up and bring it to those who are thirsty."

My hope is that this book inspires you to bring the glass to those who are thirsty—and empowers you to help them breathe easier.

DEDICATION

This book is dedicated to Nurse Bonnie, Uncle Kurt, the Stranger, Mrs. Swenson, Professor Smith, David Birch, and the many other people who, through their care and challenge, have helped me become a better person and a better leader. At the top of this list is my wife, Lily, who inspires and encourages me every day. I am deeply grateful.

This work is also dedicated to you, the reader, as you seek to be of greater service to others through the privilege of leadership.

ACKNOWLEDGMENTS

It is my great pleasure to acknowledge the support and expertise I received from many talented people in bringing this book to life.

I'm sincerely appreciative of Melanie Votaw's thoughtful line and copy editing, which strengthened the clarity of the manuscript. Many thanks also to Chris O'Byrne and Debbie O'Byrne of Jetlaunch Publishing for their skillful work on the cover design and interior layout, which captured the book's message and enhanced the reading experience. I'm also immensely grateful to Lily Corvini for the tasteful interior illustrations that added depth and character to the story of the Master Alchemist.

Finally, I extend my sincere appreciation to the many friends and colleagues who read early drafts, provided feedback, and offered encouragement along the way. This work is stronger because of your collective contributions.

REFERENCES

1   Peter F. Drucker, *The Essential Drucker: The Best of Sixty Years of Peter Drucker's Essential Writings on Management* (HarperBusiness, 2001).

2   Barbara Kellerman, *Leadership: Essential Selections on Power, Authority, and Influence* (McGraw-Hill, 2010).

3   Xenophon, *The Education of Cyrus*, trans. Wayne Ambler (Cornell University Press, 2013), xiii-xv.

4   Vivienne J. Gray, *Xenophon's Mirror of Princes: Reading the Reflections* (Oxford University Press, 2011), 1-5.

5   Michael A. Flower, "Xenophon and the Instruction of Princes," in *The Cambridge Companion to Xenophon*, edited by Michael A. Flower (Cambridge University Press, 2017), 186-188.

6   Joanne B. Ciulla, *The Heart of Leadership*, 3rd ed. (Praeger, 2004).

7   Frances Pownall, "Cyropaedia" in *The Oxford Classical Dictionary*, edited by Simon Hornblower, Antony Spawforth, and Esther Eidinow (Oxford University Press, 2012).

8   Peter Grund, "Linden, Stanton J. 2003. *The Alchemy Reader: From Hermes Trismegistus to Isaac Newton*. Cambridge: Cambridge University Press. Hard Back: ISBN 0521 63185 8; £45.00. Paperback: ISBN 0521 00000 9; £16.95," *Studia Neophilologica* 75, no. 2 (2003): 211-12. https://doi.org/10.1080/00393270310020190.

9   Alice Barnes-Brown, "Secrets of the Alchemists | All About History," *All About History Magazine*, July 26, 2018, http://www.historyanswers.co.uk/medieval-renaissance/secrets-of-the-alchemists/.

10 Lawrence Michael Principe, *The Secrets of Alchemy* (University of Chicago Press, 2013).

11 Mark S. Morrisson, *Modern Alchemy: Occultism and the Emergence of Atomic Theory* (Oxford University Press, 2007).

12 Helge Kragh, "Rutherford, Radioactivity, and the Atomic Nucleus," *arXiv*:1202.0954. Preprint, arXiv, February 5, 2012. https://doi.org/10.48550/arXiv.1202.0954.

13 John Matson, "Fact or Fiction?: Lead Can Be Turned into Gold," *Scientific American,* January 31, 2014, accessed January 5, 2026, https://www.scientificamerican.com/article/fact-or-fiction-lead-can-be-turned-into-gold/.

14 S. Acharya, A. Agarwal, G. Aglieri Rinella, et al., "Proton Emission in Ultraperipheral Pb-Pb Collisions at s N N = 5.02 TeV," *Physical Review C* 111, no. 5 (2025): 054906, https://doi.org/10.1103/PhysRevC.111.054906.

15 Society for Human Resource Management (SHRM), *SHRM Code of Ethics,* 2025, accessed January 8, 2026, https://www.shrm.org/legal/bylaws-and-code-of-ethics/code-of-ethics.

16 Denis G. Arnold and Roxanne L. Ross, "Care in Management: A Review and Justification of an Organizational Value." *Business Ethics Quarterly* 33, no. 4 (2023): 617-54, https://doi.org/10.1017/beq.2022.31.

17 Fouzia Ashfaq, Ghulam Abid, and Sehrish Ilyas, "Impact of Ethical Leadership on Employee Engagement: Role of Self-Efficacy and Organizational Commitment," *European Journal of Investigation in Health, Psychology and Education* 11, no. 3 (2021): 962-974. https://doi.org/10.3390/ejihpe11030071.

18 Dan Wang, Taiwen Feng, and Alan Lawton, "Linking Ethical Leadership with Firm Performance: A Multi-Dimensional Perspective," *Journal of Business Ethics* 145, no. 1 (2017): 95-109, https://doi.org/10.1007/s10551-015-2905-9.

19 Sonia Udod, Ibrahim Jahun, Pamela Elizabeth Baxter, et al., "Health System Leadership for Psychological Health and Organizational Resilience During the COVID-19 Pandemic: Protocol for a Multimethod Study," *JMIR Research Protocols* 14, no. 1 (2025): e66402, https://doi.org/10.2196/66402.

20 Jen Fisher, Sue Cantell, Dr. Jay Bhatt, et al., "The Important Role of Leaders in Advancing Human Sustainability," *Deloitte Insights*, June 18, 2024, accessed January 5, 2026. https://www.deloitte.com/us/en/insights/topics/talent/workplace-well-being-research-2024.html.

21 Gallup, Inc., "U.S. Employee Engagement Sinks to 10-Year Low," *Gallup.Com*, January 14, 2025, accessed January 31, 2026, https://www.gallup.com/workplace/654911/employee-engagement-sinks-year-low.aspx.

22 Um E. Rubbab, Sana Aroos Khattak, Hina Shahab, et al., "Impact of Organizational Dehumanization on Employee Knowledge Hiding," *Frontiers in Psychology* 13 (February 2022): 803905, https://doi.org/10.3389/fpsyg.2022.803905.

23 Xiuli Tang and Yingkang Gu, "Influence of Leaders' Emotional Labor and Its Perceived Appropriateness on Employees' Emotional Labor," *Behavioral Sciences* 14, no. 5 (2024): 413, https://doi.org/10.3390/bs14050413.

24 Greaves Jean, *Team Emotional Intelligence 2.0: The Four Essential Skills of High Performing Teams* (TalentSmart, 2022).

25 Mladen Adamovic, "Breaking Down Power Distance into 5 Dimensions," *Personality and Individual Differences* 208 (July 2023): 112178, https://doi.org/10.1016/j.paid.2023.112178.

26 Aeshah Abdullah Alasmari, Raseel Abdulaziz Awad, Abdulmajeed Mohamed Alshowair, et al, "Emotional Intelligence and Leadership Styles Among Managers in Primary Healthcare Centers, Riyadh, Saudi Arabia," *Journal of Healthcare Leadership* 17 (2025): 285-95, https://doi.org/10.2147/JHL.S522197.

27 Christina Maslach, Wilmar B. Schaufeli, and Michael P. Leiter, "Job Burnout." *Annual Review of Psychology* 52, no. 1 (2001): 397-422, https://doi.org/10.1146/annurev.psych.52.1.397.

28 Donald Jeanmonod, Jennifer Irick, Adam R. Munday, et al., "Compassion Fatigue in Emergency Medicine: Current Perspectives," *Open Access Emergency Medicine: OAEM* 16 (July 2024): 167-81, https://doi.org/10.2147/OAEM.S418935.

29 Joachim Stoeber and Lavinia E. Damian, "Perfectionism in Employees: Work Engagement, Workaholism, and Burnout," edited by Fuschia M. Sirois and Danielle S. Molnar, *Springer International Publishing*, 2016, https://doi.org/10.1007/978-3-319-18582-8_12.

30 Manuel Manuel, Judith Volmer, Jetmir Zyberaj, et al., "Gaining Feedback Acceptance: Leader-Member Attachment Style and Psychological Safety," *Human Resource Management Review* 33, no. 2 (2023): 100953. https://doi.org/10.1016/j.hrmr.2023.100953.

31 Delroy L. Paulhus and Kevin M Williams, "The Dark Triad of Personality: Narcissism, Machiavellianism, and Psychopathy," *Journal of Research in Personality* 36, no. 6 (2002): 556-563, https://doi.org/10.1016/S0092-6566(02)00505-6.

32 Giulia Sciotto and Francesco Pace, "The Role of Surface Acting in the Relationship between Job Stressors, General Health and Need for Recovery Based on the Frequency of Interactions at Work," *International Journal of Environmental Research and Public Health* 19, no. 8 (2022): 4800, https://doi.org/10.3390/ijerph19084800.

33 Lixia Yao, Jie Gao, Chengye Chen, et al., "How Does Emotional Labor Impact Employees' Perceptions of Well-Being? Examining the Mediating Role of Emotional Disorder," *Sustainability* 11, no. 23 (2019): 6798, https://doi.org/10.3390/su11236798.

34 A.A. Grandey, "'When 'The Show Must Go On': Surface Acting and Deep Acting as Determinants of Emotional Exhaustion and PeerRated Service Delivery," *Academy of Management Journal* 46, no. 1 (2003): 86-96, https://doi.org/10.2307/30040678.

35 Ana Patrícia Duarte, Neuza Ribeiro, Ana Suzete Semedo, et al., "Authentic Leadership and Improved Individual Performance: Affective Commitment and Individual Creativity's Sequential Mediation," *Frontiers in Psychology* 12 (May 2021): 675749, https://doi.org/10.3389/fpsyg.2021.675749.

36 Xu Li and Jianyu Zhang, "Authentic Leadership, Perceived Insider Status, Error Management Climate, and Employee Resilience: A Cross-Level Study," *Frontiers in Psychology* 13 (September 2022), https://doi.org/10.3389/fpsyg.2022.938878.

37 Vitor Hugo Silva, Ana Patrícia Duarte, Joana Palmeira Oliveira, "How Does Authentic Leadership Boost Work Engagement? Exploring the Mediating Role of Work Meaningfulness and Work-Family Enrichment," *Administrative Sciences* 13, no. 10 (2023): 219, https://doi.org/10.3390/admsci13100219.

38 Jeremias J. De Klerk, "The High Impact Leader: Moments Matter in Accelerating Authentic Leadership Development," *The Southern African Journal of Entrepreneurship and Small Business Management* 1, no. 1 (2008): 94, https://doi.org/10.4102/sajesbm.v1i1.10.

39 Brett S. Torrence and Shane Connelly, "Emotion Regulation Tendencies and Leadership Performance: An Examination of Cognitive and Behavioral Regulation Strategies," *Frontiers in Psychology* 10 (July 2019): 1486, https://doi.org/10.3389/fpsyg.2019.01486.

40 Robert M. Arnold, Anthony L. Back, Elise C. Carey, et al., *Navigating Communication with Seriously Ill Patients: Balancing Honesty with Empathy and Hope*, 2nd ed. (Cambridge University Press, 2024).

41 Julie W. Childers, Hailey Bulls, Robert Arnold, "Beyond the NURSE Acronym: The Functions of Empathy in Serious Illness Conversations," *Journal of Pain and Symptom Management* 65, no. 4 (2023): 375-379, https://doi.org/10.1016/j.jpainsymman.2022.11.029.

42 Lao Zu, *Tao Te Ching,* trans. D.C. Lau (Penguin Books, 1963).

43 Ana Junça Silva, António Caetano, Rita Rueff, "Daily Work Engagement Is a Process through Which Daily Micro-Events at Work Influence Life Satisfaction," *International Journal of Manpower* 44, no. 7 (2023): 1288-1306, https://doi.org/10.1108/IJM-05-2022-0214.

44 Qing Wang, Aijing Xia, Wei Zhang, et al., "How Challenge Job Demands Have Offsetting Effects on Job Performance: Through the Positive and Negative Emotions," *Frontiers in Psychology* 12 (2021): 745413, https://doi.org/10.3389/fpsyg.2021.745413.

45 Tino Lesener, Burkhard Gusy, Christine Wolter, "The Job Demands-Resources Model: A Meta-Analytic Review of Longitudinal Studies," *Work & Stress* 33, no. 1 (2019): 76-103, https://doi.org/10.1080/02678373.2018.1529065.

46 Jiayan Wang, Yuanmei Lan, Chaoping Li, "Challenge-Hindrance Stressors and Innovation: A Meta-Analysis," *Advances in Psychological Science* 30, no. 4 (2022): 761-780, https://doi.org/10.3724/SP.J.1042.2022.00761.

47 Arnold B. Bakker and Evangelia Demerouti, "Job Demands-Resources Theory: Taking Stock and Looking Forward," *Journal of Occupational Health Psychology* 22, no. 3 (2017): 273-285, https://doi.org/10.1037/ocp0000056.

48 Roger Fisher, William Ury, Bruce Patton, *Getting to Yes: Negotiating Agreement Without Giving In,* 2nd ed (Penguin Books, 1991).

49 George T. Doran, "There's a S.M.A.R.T. Way to Write Management's Goals and Objectives," *Management Review* 70, no. 11 (1981): 35-36.

50 Chip Heath and Dan Heath, *Switch: How to Change Things When Change Is Hard* (Random House Business Books, 2010).

51 Korn Ferry, *Korn Ferry Leadership Architect™: Global Competency Framework*, accessed January 9, 2026, https://www.kornferry.com/capabilities/talent-suite-hcm-software/korn-ferry-assess/leadership-architect.

52 *Pride,* directed by Matthew Warchus, United Kingdom: Pathé, 2007.

53 Dwi Rahmad, Suhanda Putra, Pratami Devi, "RACI Matrix Design for Managing Stakeholders in Project Case Study of PT. XYZ," *International Journal of Innovation in Enterprise System* 5, no. 2 (2021): 122-133, https://doi.org/10.25124/ijies.v5i02.134.

54 Bernard M. Bass and Ronald E. Riggio, *Transformational Leadership* (Psychology Press, 2005).

55 Katherine A. Meese and Dan Collard, *Genfluence: How to Lead a Multigenerational Workforce* (Health Administration Press, 2025).

DISCLOSURES

This book is intended for educational and informational purposes only and does not constitute legal, financial, medical, or psychological advice. The views expressed are solely those of the author and do not necessarily reflect the views of any organizations with which the author is affiliated.

No financial compensation was received from third parties in connection with this book. Any mention of organizations, products, or services is for illustrative purposes only and does not constitute endorsement.

Some examples are based on real events. Names and certain identifying details have been changed to protect privacy. Unless otherwise noted, the circumstances and outcomes are presented generally as experienced. Any resemblance to specific individuals or organizations is unintentional unless explicitly stated.

The perspectives, frameworks, and recommendations presented in this book are informed by the author's professional experience in leadership development. Leadership outcomes depend on circumstances, context, and the exercise of judgment. Strategies and examples provided are not a substitute for expert advice tailored to specific situations. Readers are responsible for evaluating the appropriateness of any content discussed and for seeking qualified professional guidance when necessary.

ABOUT THE AUTHOR

Dr. Michael Corvini is a physician-executive and health-care leader with more than two decades of clinical experience and over 15 years in senior leadership roles. He holds a BS in Psychology with a minor in Sociology from the College of William & Mary and received an MD from SUNY Downstate College of Medicine. He completed residencies in Internal Medicine and Emergency Medicine at Yale New Haven Hospital and later earned an MBA from Louisiana State University.

Dr. Corvini practiced medicine as a board-certified Emergency Physician and Hospitalist for approximately 22 years across Connecticut, New York, North Carolina, and Tennessee before retiring from clinical practice in 2023 to focus exclusively on leadership.

Throughout his career, Dr. Corvini has held multiple executive leadership roles, successfully guiding teams through the operational and strategic complexities of the healthcare industry with a disciplined commitment to excellence. A lifelong learner with a keen interest in organizational psychology, leadership theory, behavioral economics, and strategic governance, Dr. Corvini is passionate about developing future leaders. He specializes in mentoring emerging executives and fostering the strategic foresight and emotional intelligence needed to lead effectively in today's challenging and rapidly evolving business environment.

Dr. Corvini currently serves as a Division President for a national healthcare company and lives in Knoxville, Tennessee, with his wife, Lily. Together, they enjoy hiking, trail running, skiing, sailing, travelling, cooking, learning, and helping others.

www.ingramcontent.com/pod-product-compliance
Lightning Source LLC
Chambersburg PA
CBHW021526150726
47990CB00006B/2117